KOGAN PAGE

Managing Innovation and Change in Universities and Colleges

Series Editor: Susan Weil

Introducing Change from the Top in Universities and Colleges Edited by Susan Weil

Implementing Change from Within Universities and Colleges Edited by Maria Slowey

First published in 1995

Kogan Page Limited
120 Pentonville Road
London N1 9JN

British Library Cataloguing in Publication Data

A CIP record for this book is available from the British Library.

ISBN (paperback) 0 7494 1255 0

Typeset by Saxon Graphics, Ltd
Printed and bound in Great Britain by Biddles Ltd, Guildford and King's Lynn.

Contents

Notes on Contributors

Lesley Cooke is Director of Student Guidance and Support Services at Chester College of Higher Education. The thrust of her new post is to initiate and manage the changes necessary to give an increasingly diverse student population the support and guidance they need in the changing context of higher education. Brought up in Cheshire in North Wales, she attended Bedford College of Physical Education. Having taught for a couple of years in London, she returned to study at Leeds University, taking an MA in human movement studies and her doctorate. Dually qualified as a chartered psychologist and accredited sports psychologist, she has served for several years as squad psychologist to the British and Olympic sprint kayak squads. She joined Chester College of Higher Education in 1983 and in 1992 was appointed Assistant Dean of Academic Studies.

Christine King is Pro-vice-chancellor at Staffordshire University. She came to Staffordshire from the University of Central Lancashire, at that time Lancashire Polytechnic, where she had moved from teaching history, to leading a school of history and the history of art and design and to being dean of faculty which combined art and design with the humanities, music and journalism. She has also worked for the Open University, as a full-time staff tutor and as a part-time tutor.

Christine King's first degree, master's and doctorate all combine history and theology. Her master's thesis was on medieval English pilgrimage and her doctoral thesis examines the history of five Christian sects in Nazi Germany. She has published in a number of areas. Most recently she has been involved in the work of the United States Holocaust Museum in Washington DC.

As someone active in public life and the world of further and higher education, she has an interest in issues of national policy, and of student recruitment and the widening of participation. She was a founder member and first chair of the UK's 'Through the Glass Ceiling' network which exists to support and promote the cause of women senior managers in higher education.

Geoff Layer has worked in further and higher education for a number of years. He has worked at Sheffield Hallam University for 11 years where he is currently Head of Access and Guidance. As part of this role he is responsible for the development of the university's access policy, links with colleges and the credit accumulation scheme. As a result of some of the changes referred to in his chapter he has recently established an educational guidance service within the university.

Geoff is a frequent contributor to conferences and workshops in both further and higher education. He has managed several research projects on guidance, credit accumulation, access and more recently the student experience. Part of this work includes project work for the Higher Education Quality Council development project on credit accumulation and transfer.

Rhodri Phillips is Head of Research and Strategy at the Committee of Vice-chancellors and Principals, where he is developing a long-term strategic framework for higher education. He is on secondment from his post as Deputy Vice-chancellor at South Bank University, London, where he has been responsible for resource management and external relations since 1990. He joined the Civil Service from university in 1970 and worked for 20 years in senior posts in the Department of Employment, mainly on education and training programmes. During this period, he also undertook several major organization reviews on behalf of the Prime Minister's Office. He was seconded in the mid-1980s for two years to the former Inner London Education Authority to advise on major organizational changes. He was the first secretary of the Polytechnics and Colleges Funding Council when it was set up in 1988. He writes and lectures on strategic management issues in higher education.

Peter Slee is Director of Marketing and Corporate Communications at the University of Durham. After completing his PhD in modern history at Cambridge, Peter did post-doctoral research in Manchester and Durham. His book, *Learning and a Liberal Education* won the Standing Conference on Educational Studies Prize in 1987. In 1988 he joined the CBI as head of education policy before returning to manage the new Enterprise in Higher Education (EHE) programme. In 1990 Peter became head of university relations at Aston University and returned to Durham to his present job in 1992. Peter has a keen interest in training and acts as a training consultant for the European Policy and Social Research Council (EPSRC).

Maria Slowey is Professor and Director of the Department of Adult and Continuing Education at the University of Glasgow. The department provides educational programmes for many thousands of adults, representing all sections of the community in Glasgow, and on an outreach basis across the West of Scotland.

She previously held positions as Head of the Centre for External Relations and Continuing Education at the University of Northumbria at Newcastle (which she initially joined in 1984 as Senior Lecturer in Recurrent Education), Head of an Adult Education Centre in London, Research Officer on a number of national research projects on adult education, and Research Fellow with the National Association of Adult Education in Ireland. She has served on many national and international committees relating to lifelong learning, widening access and flexibility in higher education. With a particular research interest in these topics, she has also acted as consultant to a range of bodies including the Department of Education and Science, the Organisation for Economic Co-operation and Development, the Swedish National Board of Education and the European Commission.

Freda Tallantyre is Head of Unilink at the University of Northumbria at Newcastle. This department is responsible for providing a wide range of services to facilitate entry, to offer flexible routes and to support non-traditional applicants to the university. She was educated in the North of England, then graduated with first class hons in English language and literature from the University of London in 1970. A PGCE led to a lifelong career in education, including ten years of adult education, with the University of Newcastle Adult Education Department, the Workers Educational Association and the Open University. Entering the University of Northumbria at Newcastle (Newcastle Polytechnic) in 1986.

She has since directed projects on the accreditation of work-based learning, on guidance and learner autonomy, has conducted research into what makes educational programmes enterprising, and has lead responsibility for developing a learning outcomes-based approach, and NVQs/GNVQs within the university. She has spoken and published widely on issues surrounding access, women's opportunities, credit, assessment of prior learning, enterprise and guidance and support.

Jennifer Tann is Professor of Innovation Studies, Head of the School of Continuing Studies, and Dean of the Faculty of Education and Continuing Studies at the University of Birmingham. She was previously Director of Continuing Education at the University of Newcastle upon Tyne for three years and before that, Reader at Aston University Business School. She is currently a visiting Professor in Management at the University of Newcastle upon Tyne and has held a visiting Professorship at the University of Queensland, Australia. Her research is in the management of organization and technological innovation; creativity and problem-solving. She has worked with a wide range of organizations in the public and private sectors.

Richard Taylor is Professor and Director of Adult Continuing Education at the University of Leeds. He is Secretary of the Universities Association for Continuing Education (UACE). After graduating in philosophy, politics and economics from Oxford, he worked for three years at Lancaster University before moving to Leeds in 1970. His doctorate from Leeds was on the history and politics of the British nuclear disarmament movement. He has been involved in a broad range of continuing education developments, including community education with unemployed and ethnic minority groups, continuing vocational education, part-time degree and liberal adult education provision, and social work training.

He has published several books on politics and peace studies topics but has concentrated in recent years on continuing education research areas, including books on comparative continuing education research (UK/North America and UK/India), and policy studies in continuing education and higher education. He is currently a member of the executive committee of the European Society for Research on the Education of Adults and policy adviser and quality assessor for continuing education at the University of Hong Kong.

David Thorley is Head of Mechanical Engineering and Aeronautics, Co-director of the Thermo-Fluids Engineering Research Centre and Professor of Fluid Engineering at City University, London. He began his engineering career as an apprentice in the automobile industry, followed by a period as a graduate engineer in the electricity supply industry. Since joining the academic sector he has maintained strong links with industry through consultancy and development work. He has published extensively on his work in the water, petro-chemical and nuclear power industries including some 55 technical papers and three books. He is currently a scientific adviser and representative of the European Commission for a project at the Delft Hydraulics Laboratory in the Netherlands.

Ian Todd is Deputy Principal of Newcastle College. He was previously a lecturer at Monkwearmouth College of further education and a member of the law department of Newcastle upon Tyne Polytechnic. For six years prior to moving to Newcastle College he was Assistant Dean of the Faculty of Administrative and Business Studies at New College Durham.

Ian's background is in law and his qualifications and publications are in that field. His principal interests are, however, the widening of access opportunities in further education, the related need for modification of the further education curriculum and the importance of quality systems. He has acted as a consultant to a number of colleges and has been involved in several projects relating to these areas of interest.

Lee Whitehead at the time of writing was president of the Students' Union at the University of Glamorgan. He was not a particularly attentive academic in humanities at the Polytechnic of Wales, where the majority of his time and attention was taken up as a non-sabbatical Vice-president for External Affairs at the Students' Union. After his academic career had ground to a shuddering halt he was elected Sabbatical President of the newly formed University of Glamorgan Union. During his two terms of office as President he also served as an elected officer of the National Union of Students (where he was heavily involved in the 'modernizing tendencies') and as a director on the board of the National Union of Students (Services) Ltd.

He has led sessions and presented papers at various academic conferences including *Who Pays for Higher Education?* (Lancaster University), *Employer Satisfaction* (University of Central England) and *Student Charters* (Office for Public Management) during his time as president of the Union, where he attempted to give the Union a more proactive approach to education issues. He is a committed member of the Labour Party.

Series Editor's Foreword

It is with great delight that I invite you to enter into a book that sheds so much light on the dilemmas and challenges being managed by those adopting leadership roles to produce change in today's universities and colleges.

The personal accounts in this book, as in its companion, *Introducing Change 'From the Top' in Universities and Colleges* (Weil, 1994), render transparent a wide range of interior landscapes. These contributors give us direct access to their values, feelings and distinctive perspectives on what is foreground and what is background for them in the particular circumstances of their institution and role.

Some key themes run across these accounts, and these are set out aptly by the book's editor, Maria Slowey. What I want to do here is to explore a contrast between this book – written by people in different positions of influence and authority – and its companion volume, written by chief executives.

Contributors in both volumes are concerned about stimulating and supporting significant change. They are driven by external pressures as well as their own commitments to and understandings of higher education. Those who write from a perspective of being 'at the top' are accountable for their institution's financial viability, and its use of public funds. It is therefore perhaps not surprising that those at the head of an institution tend to locate their reflections in what might be called a strategic or business paradigm. What is paramount for them is the way in which the organization can best secure its position in the new public-sector marketplace. They are preoccupied with how best to bring about changes in their institution's identity, culture, key relationships, ways of working and mission (Beckhard and Pritchard, 1992) relevant to meeting the demands of competing stakeholders. These include students, employers, professionals, politicians, and their constituent communities.

The chief executives speak about the importance of influence, persuasion and the 'winning of hearts and minds'; all the same, they are in a position of clear power and influence, with no illusions about their responsibilities. Many knew that they had only to spit and others would react as if it were a waterfall. And many felt obliged to do just this to bring about the changes that they perceived as relevant to achieving political, educational and financial viability.

In this volume, a different paradigm is emphasized. These contributors are not negligent of the accountabilities being managed by chief executives but they give far greater priority to human activity – and particularly those pluralistic forms of endeavour and spirit that characterize a university or college. The preoccupation here is how best to inspire and coordinate such activity to respond to new pressures without undermining the best of the old or the creativity, diversity and effort – individual and collegial – that characterizes an effective and vibrant university or college. As the editor of this volume puts it, what people are concerned about here is how 'people can work to the best advantage of everyone in light of changing circumstances'.

It is therefore perhaps not surprising that reflections laced with conviction and authority characterize Volume 1, whereas here we find explorations of commitment laced with value conflicts and role dilemmas.

Many of the people herein have adopted their roles because of their commitment to particular principles or because of some deeply felt dissatisfaction with the status quo. Whereas they can 'weep alongside their colleagues' for the loss of the good old days, equally they can celebrate the power of giving new meaning to tired concepts such as community, quality or student learning. I would suggest that many of these contributors are effective in bringing about transformations in their colleagues' attitudes and behaviours because of their capacity to operate on the basis of clear educational and leadership principles, which they make transparent in both words and actions. Their passions and enthusiasms, as well as their arguments, become compelling. But most importantly, so does the integrity of their position and the validity of what they are persuading people towards – irrespective of government or management policy.

All the same, what becomes evident is that those in middle management positions enter into these waters at much cost, including their own professional isolation. In this, they mirror the dilemma experienced by those colleagues who will do anything to disassociate themselves from 'managers' and 'management', however committed they may be to the changes being proposed.

The contributors' struggles with paradoxes and dilemmas of role are also illuminating in ways that differ from those identified by chief executives. Many of the contributors here have *only* influence. Others have limited authority and power. Within their institutions, they are often both 'pig in the middle' and 'eye in the storm'. A 'command and control' style is not perceived as an option (and many would argue that it seldom is, especially in a university or college). They often have no choice but to win hearts and minds. Therefore, they are preoccupied with how best to do this without becoming labelled a 'management lackey' or colluding with outcomes that they never intended to be associated with, such as in connection with some internal or external policy to which they were initially committed.

In such reflections, the finer tunes and tones of managing change from within today's universities and colleges become revealed as these contributors consider how best to move forward, in ways that seem 'right' for them as individuals, their colleagues and their particular institutions.

Our aim with this series is to provide a readable resource that will help to stimulate debate among those both effecting and being affected by significant change in universities and colleges. It is for people who are undertaking similar leadership roles, in the belief that their distinctive efforts and approaches to managing change will have meaning and a beneficial iimpact, not just on the financial bottom line but on the quality of student and staff experience.

These accounts, juxtaposed against those in the companion volume, alert us to the dangers of needlessly creating artificial managerial–professional schisms in today's universities and colleges. We must have the courage to explore new interfaces between the strategic, the educational and the human dimensions of managing change in today's universities and colleges. This book reminds us that we cannot afford to stifle leadership and potential with narrowly conceived understandings of management or administration. Unlike many books on managing change, readers will find few easy generalizations here. Instead, these contributors open us up to new possibilities for change in today's universities and colleges, when certain kinds of processes, principles and relationships are placed at the heart of the change effort. As importantly, they demonstrate how students and staff can benefit from giving new meaning to tired concepts.

REFERENCES

Beckhard, R and Pritchard, W (1993) *Changing the Essence*, San Francisco, CA: Jossey-Bass.

Weil, S (1994) *Introducing Change From the Top*, London: Kogan Page.

Preface and Acknowledgements

INTRODUCTION

It is widely acknowledged that the expansion of post-compulsory education in Britain cannot be achieved by delivering 'more of the same'. The basic premise of this volume is that although policy and funding strategies are influential in shaping the move from an elite to a mass system, it is changes *within* institutions themselves that make the real difference.

Little is known about the increasing number of those who, at various levels within universities and colleges, find themselves confronted with the task of managing these dramatic changes. The majority are men and women who have held, and may continue to hold, conventional academic positions. Most came into further and higher education with a view to pursuing teaching and research in their respective disciplines. Circumstances, however, have conspired to place them in leadership roles in relation to implementing change within their institutions.

The contributions in this volume do not claim to be representative of the entire spectrum of change affecting universities and colleges. They do, however, illustrate certain key dimensions of these changes – the development of strategies aimed at widening access; the introduction of new teaching and learning methodologies in the light of increasing student numbers and a declining unit of resource; the utilization of short-term project funding to achieve curriculum change; the responses to increased competition and accountability in relation to research; the new emphasis on generic staff development; and the more active and influential role for students in shaping the system within which they study.

Some of the contributors hold senior positions within their institutions (at pro-vice-chancellor or vice-principal levels), others illustrate how times of change can throw up opportunities for new actors (staff in relatively junior academic positions or student representatives). What all the contributors share in common is their leadership responsibility for the implementation of certain aspects of change.

This book adopts a similar approach to its companion volume edited by Susan Weil, also published by Kogan Page in 1994. *Introducing Change 'From the Top' of Universities and Colleges* explores issues of managing change from the perspective of those holding the most senior position in an institution – vice-chancellor, principal, chief executive. By reflecting on their own personal experience and practice, both books give, as Susan Weil puts it, access to '...contributors' different interior landscapes and so to their distinctive values, feelings and distinctive perspectives on what is at issue and what is not, in the enactment of their role'.

INTENDED READERSHIP

Responding to current pressures requires active leadership at *a variety of levels* within universities and colleges. We hope that this volume will provide assistance, insight and encouragement for those charged with taking on such roles across the system.

The contributions highlight some of the issues and dilemmas facing those who find themselves in what is frequently an uncomfortable position between senior management and their colleagues. We also hope, therefore, that these accounts will help vice-chancellors and principals to more fully appreciate the importance of support 'from the top' and peers and colleagues at other levels to appreciate the importance of avoiding an automatic reaction against the introduction of any change, evaluating each development in its own right.

In addition, these accounts offer valuable material to those with a more academic interest in the nature of cultural change within large institutions, and/or the relevance of different leadership styles. While they are located within a British (and, for various reasons, largely English) context, the nature of the forces with which these accounts are grappling are common across the post-compulsory education systems of Western societies.

ACKNOWLEDGEMENTS

The core of this book comprises accounts and reflections of people who (with greater and lesser degrees of arm-twisting!) agreed to share their experiences with a wider audience. Some were familiar and comfortable with this approach, particularly those who had previously had some involvement in helping students to identify learning gained from experience, and those who were acquainted with the concept of the *reflective practitioner*. For others, reflecting on educational and leadership processes as opposed to academic work in their own discipline was something very new.

I am extremely grateful to all for joining in this venture. The insights offered by contributors are always interesting, stimulating and, on occasion, controversial. The reader will appreciate their candour – although in some situations the names have been changed to protect the innocent! Their commitment to achieving the best outcome for colleagues and students, in often difficult circumstances, is evident and was the main motivating factor for contributors agreeing to share their experiences with others. It has been a great pleasure for me to work again with those whom I already knew, and to get to know others whom I had previously only known by reputation. I hope all friendships will survive the experience!

I would like to pay particular tribute to Susan Weil, editor of the companion volume to this, and overall editor of the series. The original conception for the series was Susan's, based on her research on experiential learning, and her extensive consultancy work with a wide range of universities and colleges. Intensive discussions with Susan were invaluable, particularly in the early stages, and there were many times when her energy levels and enthusiasm were essential to keep momentum going! We both also enjoyed encouragement from Helen Carley of Kogan Page, and her successor, Clare Andrews. I am grateful to Julie Nielson and Katharine Lilley in Glasgow, both of whom provided me with professional secretarial support of the highest standard. Finally, I wish to express my appreciation for the forbearance and support of many colleagues in relation to my own attempts at initiating and implementing change.

Maria Slowey
Glasgow
December 1994

PART ONE:

INTRODUCTION

Chapter 1

Reflections on Change – Academics in Leadership Roles

Maria Slowey

INTRODUCTION

This book is about reflections – the critical self-assessment and questioning of management practice by people who, in different ways, have responsibility for leading and implementing change within further and higher education institutions. Most were not trained as managers and started their careers as 'traditional' academics. It is not an easy transformation and none of those who have made the change underestimate the costs. As an academic, the primary focus of intellectual concern is discipline-centred, but as a manager or 'change agent', the academic discipline becomes secondary. Those who swap roles and make the transition end up with new perspectives and outlooks. Their priorities are altered and they often encounter opposition from a less than supportive academic community which, despite its commitment to a search for new knowledge, can be conservative when it comes to new ways of working.

Charged with implementing change, the academic as manager must redefine his or her role. It is for most people a personal challenge and it is also a challenge for the institution as a whole. Change in itself is neither good nor bad; what matters is the kind of change. The reflections of the various contributors will, hopefully, shed some light on the dramatic and profound changes currently affecting further and higher education and the strategies being adopted to respond to external forces in a positive and proactive way.

There are no simple blueprints for success. However, by offering reflections on strategies which worked, and some which did not, it is hoped to contribute to the broader understanding of the nature of the management of change in the complex environment of further and higher education, and to provide support to the increasing numbers of the academic community placed in positions of implementing change within their own institutions.

THE POLICY CONTEXT

To say that both the pace and the nature of change in post-compulsory education in Britain over the past decade have been dramatic is an understatement. Change within further and higher education has been almost without parallel in terms of the explosion of student numbers, levels and methods of resourcing, quality control systems, the curriculum and modes of study.[1] The outcome has been, as Trow (1994, p.11) puts it, '...a more profound re-orientation than any other system in industrial societies'. These changes have placed tremendous pressures on traditional academic cultures and styles of administration. Two particular effects have been highlighted by Scott (1993). In the first place there is a loss of academic intimacy and the emergence of a new cadre of academic managers. Secondly, there is an increasing tendency towards radical devolution from the centre of institutions to operational units – with an accompanying impact on leadership requirements at the departmental level.

The factors which have led to this 'profound reorientation' are not difficult to discern, deriving largely from a political climate which emphasizes 'value for money' and radical reform of all aspects of the public sector. It was these objectives which shaped government policy following the 1979 election. While higher education took steps to introduce reform from within the system – through, for example, the work of the Committee of Vice-Chancellors and Principals on efficiency in higher education (CVCP, 1985) – the government proceeded to pursue its policies through legislation and a variety of funding strategies. (Readers should refer to the Appendix for a more detailed account of the policy context and the nature of its impact on the system.)

The essential features of the new agenda for higher education which influenced subsequent developments were set out in the White Paper *Higher Education: Meeting the Challenge* (DES, 1987). Largely as a result of concerns about international competitiveness there was a major emphasis on (i) expansion of the system by increasing the age participation rate (that is, the percentage of young people staying on in education beyond the compulsory school leaving age); (ii) widening access to young people with qualifications other than A Levels (Advanced Levels) and (iii) offering new opportunities to mature students. Links with employers and labour market requirements provided a secondary series of themes including continuing part-time education for those in employment who wished to improve their professional knowledge and skills. The policy framework also placed considerable emphasis on

- improvements in the design and content of courses and the quality of teaching;
- external measures of quality in research; and
- increased efficiency of institutions as measured by various performance indicators.

The drive to increase efficiency and the utilization of external measures of quality was rapidly taken further as the Education Reform Act (1988) was followed by another White Paper in 1991, *Higher Education: A New Framework* (DfE, 1991) and by even more radical legislative changes in the Further and Higher Education Act (1992). The latter introduced separate Higher Education Funding Councils (HEFCs) in England, Wales and Scotland, funding all higher education institutions in those countries; polytechnics were awarded university status (the abolition of the 'binary divide'); new quality assurance methods were introduced, including a quality assurance role for the HEFCs, and a quality audit unit developed by the universities.

In addition to these legislative changes, another important strategy employed to effect change in further and higher education has been through the use of targeted funding. As the core unit of resource diminished over the period in question, institutions were encouraged to bid for short-term funding made available for development work in support of policy priorities. There is, of course, an irony in a Conservative government firmly committed to market principles adopting such overtly interventionist strategies. As Duke points out:

> *The paradox of a strongly directive and centralising Administration wedded in principle to the free play of market forces is well displayed in the education sector, and curiously echoes the behaviour of mid-Victorian administrations in the heyday of laissez-faire (Duke, 1988, p.31).*

In particular, the use of additional funds on the basis of competitive bids has been an important instrument in locating further and higher education closer to the sphere of the training infrastructure. It is significant that the bulk of these funds has been channelled through the government department responsible for the labour market and vocational training (the Employment Department) rather than that responsible for education (in England, the Department for Education, in Scotland, the Scottish Office Education Department). While acknowledging the 'inescapably societal character' (Barnett, 1990) of higher education, these types of initiatives reflected the dominant interests of the world of work in a new and more explicit way.

One of the most significant of these targeted initiatives in the higher education sector of the late 1980s was Enterprise in Higher Education (EHE). As several of the chapters in this volume point out, this particular initiative was initially greeted with considerable suspicion, if not outright hostility, because it was seen as an attempt at direct ideological intervention in the curriculum – an arrow directed at the academic heart of universities and colleges. However, the level of funding was attractive (in the region of £1m for larger institutions) and most institutions eventually submitted bids, although the decision to do so was by no means always uncontroversial and was frequently accompanied by much internal debate. The reasons for the strength of feeling are not difficult to discern. Institutions were being offered an inducement to undertake curriculum development in line with government policies – with a particular stress on transferable skills and strengthened links with employers. On the other hand, advocates of EHE within institutions argued that the funding could be used to introduce changes which had long been desirable for sound educational reasons, in particular in relation to supporting steps to widen access to a broader section of the population.

With this combination of legislative and funding strategies, by 1994, the government,

> *...saw itself as having 'solved' the issue of higher education. The sector had been reorganized, numbers of students had grown, and issues of quality were being addressed. As the government saw it, the onus was now on the universities and colleges themselves – cajoled by the HEFCs – to make a mass higher education system work efficiently and effectively (Appendix).*

National policies undoubtedly set the broad parameters but, as Wagner (1989) puts it, the real 'action' takes place at the *institutional* level. The importance of the institutional dimension is evidenced by the different responses that universities and colleges display despite the fact that they all operate within the same policy context.

These institutional responses have to be managed. This volume contains the personal accounts of a number of those who are centrally involved in this task of assisting their institutions not only to survive, but hopefully to make progress towards the achievement of their respective missions, within this very difficult policy environment.

THE NATURE OF THE TASK FACING AGENTS OF CHANGE

Who are the men and women in universities and colleges who have the job of delivering this 'efficient' and 'effective' system, while still ensuring that the fundamental values of higher education are at least maintained, if not enhanced? Who are these people who have to take leadership roles in times of dramatic changes in both student numbers and diversity of the student body? Who are the people who have to implement new quality systems in teaching and research at a time of a radical reduction in the unit of resource? What training do they have? What are their backgrounds and values? How do they cope with what appears to be constant change and uncertainty? How do they reconcile traditional academic values with those of a political regime which frequently seems to hold such values in contempt? And perhaps the most important question of all – why do they do it?

It is with a view to answering some of these questions that ten people who, in very different ways, are involved in implementing and managing change in the further and higher education sector, were approached to tell their 'personal stories'. It is a great tribute to all that they have agreed to share with a wider audience their reflections of the strategies which they have adopted in seeking to shape and control their environment for the benefit of students, colleagues and their institutions. They have been willing to describe what has worked and, perhaps more importantly, what has not worked! They come from different discipline backgrounds and are in different structural positions. Some have senior management roles across their institutions; others are heads of departments; others have no budgets, no managerial authority but act as 'change agents' on a variety of fronts; and one is president of a Student's Union. What all share in common, and this comes through very forcibly in their accounts, is a deep commitment to doing all they can to assist their respective institutions to best cope with fundamental change in a proactive rather than reactive way.

This volume does not set out to provide tidy 'how to' tips for those concerned with managing and implementing change in universities and colleges. Instead it offers the considered reflections of people who have, in their different ways, had responsibility for introducing change at some level within their institution. Few of them received formal training in management techniques, and a phrase which recurs is 'learning on the hoof'. Just how valuable formal management training is, in any case, has long been a subject of heated debate – although many of the contributors acknowledge the lack of formal management training as a perceived handicap which they had to overcome.

As has been argued above, the motive force behind the profound changes that further and higher education have experienced in recent years has been largely political. Almost inevitably, therefore, the managers of change on occasion find themselves in the position of actively implementing government policies. They may well feel less than comfortable with many aspects of these policies but, as the ten accounts in this book reveal, such people see an important part of their role as responding to these external pressures in a positive way, with a view to at least mitigating their worst effects, and at best achieving educationally desirable outcomes. The fact that they are required to implement many government policies and initiatives to which there is a fair measure of hostility amongst their academic peers makes the whole endeavour even more difficult. Most academics would prefer to be left in peace so that they could get on with their research and teaching. To someone whose major professional preoccupation is the refinement of a rarefied theory in nuclear physics, many of the interventions by central government are regarded as unnecessary and unwelcome. Those responsible for leading change, who have themselves typically held (and may still hold) conventional academic positions, therefore find themselves with a role that is not only inherently difficult in itself, as is any kind of management role, but which is also subject to concerns about possible compromise on traditional academic values.

Many of the contributors point to the particular difficulties and challenges of seeking to lead and implement change within academic institutions in contrast to being a manager in industry or commerce. Handy (1993), in his overview of research on issues relating to organizational culture and change, uses the stereotype of the professor to illustrate the professional who would prefer to be operating in a minimalist organizational structure:

> *He (sic) does what he has to, teaches what he must, in order to retain his position in that organisation. But essentially he regards the organisation as a base on which he can build his own career, carry out his own interests, all of which may indirectly add interest to the organisation though that would not be the point of doing them (p.191).*

He then goes on to comment, with some degree of understatement, that individuals with this orientation are 'not easy to manage' – a point which comes through in the case studies. While this volume was not designed to make a theory, the accounts do shed light on strategies for leading and managing academic staff.

Part of the difficulty arises from lack of clarity about the role of the 'academic manager'. As Tann (Chapter 6) points out from her extensive staff development work with heads of departments, not only are many such appointments short-term and, particularly in the older universities, are rarely accompanied by a detailed job description, but the nature of the managerial responsibility for other academic colleagues is itself very vague. It is perhaps not surprising, therefore, that contributors intuitively find their way to utilizing some of the best management techniques of persuasion, team building and – a recurrent theme – 'ownership'.

As King (Chapter 2) emphasizes, the essence of academic training is to promote critical thinking and a questioning of authority. On a bad day an academic manager seeking to promote some form of change may feel that organizing academics is, as Thorley (Chapter 3) puts it, akin to herding cats! It is particularly difficult when the area of change which is being pursued is one which at times may seem to complement the policies of an apparently hostile government. Many contributors reflect in some detail on the very real conflicts they have experienced about the extent to which promotion of certain kinds of change can be seen to be 'playing into the politicians' hands'. This can apply to initiatives which are being pursued for the best of educational reasons, for example, strategies aimed at widening access to sections of the population traditionally under-represented in higher education.

Nevertheless, higher education does have a wider social function which transcends the preoccupations of individual academics – participation rates in the UK *are* low, many barriers to access *do* exist, some modes of study *are* inflexible, sometimes teaching practices *can be* antiquated, and quality, as seen from the students' perspective, *may not* always have been given the prominence it deserves. Furthermore, resource levels in certain parts of the system *were* relatively generous.

In this context, traditional distinctions between Left and Right break down. Robertson (1994), in a major report on the introduction of more flexible credit systems in higher education sponsored by the Higher Education Quality Council, argues that 'radical' positions of both Left and Right tend to share a similar diagnosis of the problems of the British economy and aspects of higher education. In other words, he suggests that the outlook of the 'radicals' of the Left and Right have a lot in common with each other, and these can be contrasted with the alternative perspective of the 'romantics' of both the Left and Right, which also have much in common with each other. Robertson puts it succinctly:

> *...there appears to be a common radical agenda across the political spectrum to introduce greater flexibility and student choice, to encourage markets within higher education and to expand access. This is likely to embrace student loans, a personal commitment and an acceptance that professional academic sovereignty should not remain a barrier to the achievement of these objectives (p.334).*

The position of what he calls the 'romantics' of both the Left and the Right, he suggests, appears to be a search for an earlier 'golden age' of higher education, '...when academics had time to engage their preferences and when everyone knew standards were being maintained' (p.334).

Whatever we may think about particular government policies, further and higher education cannot and should not be immune to change. Someone has to implement and manage that change. It is not easy, it does not always work, sometimes it causes more problems than it solves. However, the alternative to proactively responding to change and attempting to manage it, is to be engulfed by new policies and initiatives without having any control over how they unfold and develop. This is essentially the lesson of the ten accounts in this volume.

COMMON THEMES EMERGING FROM THE TEN ACCOUNTS

The contributors to this volume hold different positions within their respective institutions and reflect on their experiences of managing very different aspects of change in further and higher education – developing a research strategy for a new department; implementing cross-institutional policies in relation to areas such as widening access or the introduction of comprehensive guidance support for students; introducing new teaching and learning methodologies in order to deal with vastly increased student populations; overseeing the implementation of externally funded initiatives; introducing a total quality management (TQM) approach into a department; identifying the staff development needs of heads of departments; contributing, from a Students' Union perspective, to the strategic planning of an institution. However, while the focus of attention of each of the chapters is quite different, certain common themes do emerge very strongly. Five of these are highlighted below.

The stimulus for change

Undoubtedly one of the main factors leading to many of the changes described, particularly for heads of departments and those with resource management responsibility, can be traced directly to resource issues. Slee (Chapter 5), for example, describes how a decrease in the departmental budget of 12 per cent prompted his department to undertake a major internal review. Thorley's department (Chapter 3) was 'down-sized' from 46 academic staff to about half that number, while at the same time being under pressure to demonstrate enhanced research productivity. Todd (Chapter 9), as vice-principal of a large college of further education, was facing the academic implications of a declining unit of resource and increased student numbers.

In other cases the stimulus for change resulted indirectly from new funding mechanisms. For example, Taylor (Chapter 4) describes how changes in the funding methodology for continuing education prompted his department to explore the possibility of a greater involvement in mainstream university activities relating to widening access and part-time degrees. Similarly, Layer (Chapter 8) points to an anticipated shift by the Funding Councils to funding on an output-based model as the key factor which stimulated his institution to consider a greater emphasis on student retention and student guidance and support services.

A third way in which funding acts as a stimulus for change is through the opportunity offered by external resources to support particular development activities. Tallantyre (Chapter 7) points to the timely nature of the Enterprise in Higher Education initiative which provided additional resources to undertake certain desired developments which otherwise might not have got off the ground or which certainly would have progressed at a slower rate. Others also describe how in some cases relatively small amounts of money are sufficient to induce change in certain areas.

Strategies adopted in implementing change

Two chapters explicitly focus on the question of strategy in relation to the implementation of change. Tann (Chapter 6) identifies the general staff development requirements of heads of departments as they seek to manage major transformations in the context of great uncertainty. Slee (Chapter 5) describes the utilization of one particular approach to change, TQM, within one particular department. All the other chapters address questions of strategy more generally from within the context of specific examples of seeking to introduce particular types of change.

Whether the focus is explicitly strategic or not, certain common phrases recur in all contributions:

- building trust,
- winning hearts and minds,
- getting ownership of change,
- team building,
- honesty.

What comes through clearly in all accounts is the necessity for those leading change to be convinced on a personal level about the value of a particular initiative. Once convinced of its value, they put tremendous effort into seeking to bring their colleagues along with them. They talk about the importance of gaining allies, both at senior management levels within their institutions and at the 'grass roots' levels, and several contributors point to the fact that on occasion their most vociferous colleagues end up as some of their strongest supporters once convinced of the benefits of the proposed changes.

Many of the chapters stress the importance of task groups, working groups, or what Whitehead (Chapter 11) refers to as 'slice groups'. These dynamic group structures are seen as efficient ways of making progress in relation to the implementation of change and gaining ownership. What is interesting is that such groups frequently cut across traditional hierarchical, discipline or functional divisions. They typically involve academic, administrative and other support staff, and – most radical of all – students on a genuine, rather than token, basis. They are also very different to traditional institutional committees in that, as Tallantyre (Chapter 7) describes them, they are given a remit 'to act rather than report' and are wound up when their action is no longer necessary.

Other strategies adopted with a view to achieving the desired trust and ownership include 'away days', developing personal contact by, for example, inviting colleagues to one's home, and a host of more generalized attempts to deepen the level of interaction between all interested parties.

Costs and benefits to the individual

Given some of the trials and tribulations described in these chapters and the effort involved in moving forward and implementing change, one wonders why the contributors do not settle for the 'quiet life'. While in one sense the answers to this question are as diverse as the individuals represented in this volume, in another sense a clear pattern can be discerned. Although some people describe how they fortuitously ended up in situations where they have responsibility for implementing change, the fact is that all describe the importance of having a deep personal commitment to the changes which they are seeking to promote. All of the contributors are in some sense *leaders*, in that they are people who have a view of how to move forward and they wish to communicate this view to others. It is worth mentioning that this conception of leadership has no necessary relationship to organizational hierarchies.

While there may be career rewards for the individual in adopting this leadership role, the overwhelming motivation appears to lie in a strong desire to shape the nature of the environment in which people work to the best advantage of everyone in the light of changing circumstances.

The costs of this role are also alluded to by many contributors. There can be feelings of isolation and self-doubt, particularly so given the controversial policy context described earlier in this chapter. While many continue to teach, undoubtedly the opportunity for contact with students is reduced simply as a result of pressures on time and the accumulation of administrative responsibilities. Opportunities to conduct research are also severely curtailed for people in these positions. This is a major area of concern for many contributors and for the many other heads of department described in Tann's chapter. King speaks for many when she writes:

> *Like many other teachers/researchers turned managers, I have had to face losses; of students, of sabbaticals, of 'serious' research and of a large cohort of colleagues. Pursuit of my 'subject' has become my hobby. The benefits are that it is possible to effect change on a much wider scale than before and I can introduce what I believe are real benefits for the work of students and teachers. Not everyone wants to do this job, but most academics believe they could do a better job given half the chance (Chapter 2).*

Poacher turned gamekeeper?

The tensions between the autonomy of the individual academic and increasing tendencies towards cross-institutional policies and the development of a more collective ethos have already been raised in this chapter. Several contributors describe their own transition from that of a 'traditional' academic vigorously defending their autonomy, to a position where they recognize the necessity of shared and collective approaches whether for positive reasons or simply for survival. They also point out that a self-awareness of the views and perspectives which they previously held enables them to understand more fully the outlooks of some of their colleagues. Cooke, for example, expresses her personal reorientation as follows: for much of her career she was so bound up with the perceptions and pressures of the 'ordinary lecturer' that it took a long time to appreciate that her personal beliefs in fact fitted the underlying principles of the College mission (serving the community, equality of opportunity, maintenance of quality, striving for excellence) breaking down the 'us' and 'them' distinctions. As Layer and others point out, this self-awareness is of considerable assistance in gaining credibility with other colleagues. Some contributors have even had the experience of being head of a 'barony' which they vigorously defended against perceived interference from the centre of the institution! As Taylor highlights, there is a continuing problem of proper demarcations between the centre and the periphery, between institutional and departmental functions. In this context, several of the chapters highlight the changing culture which has been created as a result of increasing transparency of funding arrangements within institutions and, in particular, devolved budgeting. In fact, much of what the contributors to this volume are describing directly relates to these issues.

A fresh perspective

It is interesting to note how many of the contributors make direct reference to the fact that they were in a new position, coming from a slightly different background, or in some way or other an 'outsider'. Slee, for example, was the 'new kid in town' when, as director of a central academic support service, he was faced with responding to a major cut in budget and a change of function. Tallantyre refers to the ideas and approaches which she brought to higher education from her background in adult education. Whitehead and his colleagues in the Students' Union produced a strategic plan for his university which had a fundamental effect on the eventual university plan – many of the individual recommendations produced by the students were subsequently included in the formal submission to the Funding Council. Thorley had a background in industry before coming into higher education, while Cooke explicitly refers to herself as something of an 'outsider'. In Taylor's case, he was head of a continuing education department, and while such departments have traditionally played a very important role at the interface between universities and the broader community, in the past they frequently were not at the heart of the mainstream activities of institutions.

There is also the important question of gender. With women significantly under-represented at many levels of institutional hierarchies, they have far less to lose from change and may well see change as providing invaluable new opportunities for women students and staff. Certainly several of the contributors point to the fact that women sometimes appear to be more comfortable with change than their male counterparts – not because of any inherent differences but simply because they have less of a stake in the existing system.

STRUCTURE OF THIS VOLUME

The contributions in this volume address different dimensions of change in further and higher education and as such can stand as individual accounts in their own right. However, in order to focus the reader's attention on the common themes and issues which emerge, they have been grouped into three parts, each of which is introduced by an editorial comment. The chapters in *Part Two – Leading Change, Heads of Departments and Others,* focuses on issues to do with implementing change from the very important leadership position of head of a division or department, or equivalent sub-unit within an institution. However, in order to establish the broader picture, the contributions commence with *Christine King's* reflections which cover her experience of leading change from the position of head of department, then dean of faculty and, currently, pro-vice-chancellor. This range of experience gives her particularly valuable insights into different dimensions of leading change at different levels within the hierarchy of an institution. Following this 'illustrative account', the next chapters focus more specifically on leadership of change from the position of someone who is head of a unit, division, or department. *David Thorley* presents two very interesting cases where he was in a leadership position promoting major changes which had as their objective the enhancement of research activity. He highlights those factors which resulted in one exercise achieving a more successful outcome than the other. *Richard Taylor*, as head of a department of adult and continuing education, provides a detailed analysis of the dilemmas facing heads of departments as they seek to promote the best interests of their departments in the context of broader institutional and external changes. Utilizing a number of examples he reflects on the effectiveness of different strategies in implementing change. *Peter Slee* reflects on the processes and issues involved in utilizing one particular strategy for the implementation of change – TQM – in the context of a central academic support department. While in one respect a commitment to one particular approach was a bold choice, this account stresses its flexibility and relevance to many situations in academic institutions. In the final contribution in this part, *Jennifer Tann* draws upon her extensive experience of involvement in staff development work with those holding leadership positions, mainly at the head of department level. Based on this experience, and her own direct involvement as head of department in several universities, she identifies eight central issues which heads of departments have to address in implementing change.

The central importance of strategic planning in recent years for universities and colleges has led to an increased emphasis on cross-institutional policies. The accounts in *Part Three – Implementing Cross-Institutional Change* offer examples of implementing change in three particular areas of policy. Freda Tallantyre reflects on her experience directing an Enterprise in Higher Education initiative. This account graphically highlights the impact of external funding and the strategies which were adopted – with considerable success – to overcome initial concerns and, in some quarters, hostility to the project. A second example is provided by *Geoff Layer* who, along with his colleagues, sought to persuade others in his institution of the importance of introducing a comprehensive educational guidance and support service for students. In this case no additional resources were available to introduce these changes so a variety of strategies had to be adopted to convince budget-holders that it was in their interests to transfer resources from other areas to this new activity. The third chapter in this section is by *Ian Todd*, vice-principal of a large college of further education. His account reflects the importance of creative thinking as colleges and universities come under increasing financial pressures to teach large and increasingly diverse groups of students. An important aspect of the role of people in such positions is, he suggests, to identify new teaching and learning approaches which at least should not lead to a diminution of the student experience and at best may lead to its enhancement.

The contributions in *Part Four – Opportunities for New Actors in Times of Change*, have been selected to illustrate how times of change can throw up opportunities for new actors on the scene. In the first example, *Lesley Cooke* describes how a temporary developmental position, outside the conventional institutional hierarchy, placed her in a position to act as a change agent on a number of interrelated areas. With little or no resources at her disposal and little or no authority to fall back on, the strategies which she adopted to implement change relied to a considerable extent on her own ingenuity. Finally, it is perhaps appropriate that the last word in this volume should be given to a student representative – *Lee Whitehead*. The traditional role of students in the running of an institution has tended to involve either token membership of university or college committees, or the 'opposition voice', frequently channelled through the Students' Union. This chapter offers a reflective (and most entertaining!) account of the dilemmas facing those who make the choice to take responsibility for seeking to control change.

A FINAL WORD ABOUT EXPERIENTIAL LEARNING

These contributions do not claim to be definitive. However, they do address important issues of wider general concern without being anecdotal.[2] In this respect each contributor, to a certain extent, demonstrates the characteristics of a *reflective practitioner* (Schön, 1983). Rather than writing a theoretical exposition on an area of debate in their field, or reporting on the results of new experiments, contributors were asked to place their experiences in managing change directly at the centre of their accounts. They were asked to reflect and analyse their own role and experiences in relation to the implementation of change, and to try and draw out the lessons they have learnt from that experience.

The value of the insights produced by this approach speaks for itself in the following chapters.

NOTES

1. In addition to material contained under references, for useful overviews of recent trends see, for example, O Fulton (ed.) (1989) *Access and Institutional Change,* Milton Keynes, SRHE/Open University Press; G Parry and C Wake (eds) (1990) *Access and Alternative Futures,* London, Hodder and Stoughton; T Schuller (ed.) (1991) *The Future of Higher Education*, Milton Keynes, SRHE/Open University Press; C Duke (1992) *The Learning University: Towards a Paradigm?*, Milton Keynes, SRHE/Open University Press; I McNay (ed.) (1992) *Visions of Post-Compulsory Education*, Milton Keynes, SRHE/Open University Press.
2. For an introduction to experiential learning see for example, S Weil and I McGill (eds) (1989) *Making Sense of Experiential Learning: Diversity in Theory and Practice*, Milton Keynes, SRHE/Open University Press, or N Evans (1992) *Experiential Learning – Assessment and Accreditation*, London, Routledge.

REFERENCES

Barnett, R (1990) *The Idea of Higher Education*, Milton Keynes: SRHE/Open University Press.

Committee of Vice-Chancellors and Principals (1985) *Report of the Steering Committee on Efficiency Studies in Universities*, London: CVCP.

Department for Education (1991) *Higher Education: A New Framework,* London: HMSO.

Department of Education and Science (1987) *Higher Education: Meeting the Challenge,* London: HMSO.

Duke, C (1988) 'Adults into higher education: trends and issues in the United Kingdom', in Abrahamson, K, Rubenson, K and Slowey, M *Adults in the Academy: International trends in adult and higher education*, Stockholm: Swedish National Board of Education.

Handy, C (1993) *Understanding Organizations*, (4th edn), Harmondsworth: Penguin.

Robertson, D (1994) *Choosing to Change – Extending access, choice and mobility in higher education,* London: Higher Education Quality Council.

Schön, DAC (1983) *The Reflective Practitioner: How professionals think in action*, New York: Basic Books.

Scott, P (1993) 'The idea of the university in the twenty-first century: a British perspective' in the *British Journal of Educational Studies*, 41, 1.

Trow, M (1994) *Managerialism and the Academic Profession: Quality and control*, London: Open University Quality Support Centre.

Wagner, L (1989) 'National policy and institutional development', in Fulton, O (ed.), *Access and Institutional Change,* Milton Keynes: SRHE/Open University Press.

PART TWO:

LEADING CHANGE – HEADS OF DEPARTMENT AND OTHERS

EDITORIAL COMMENT

To set the scene for this section of the book, the contributions begin with Christine King's reflections on her experience of implementing change across a spectrum of different leadership positions in different institutions. This range of experience places her in a strong position to draw out the issues and varying perspectives involved in coping with change at a variety of management levels. Her initial experience of leading a department in a potentially hostile national context was, she suggests, invaluable in helping her to appreciate some of the resistance which she now encounters in implementing change at an institutional level as pro-vice-chancellor. While providing a graphic account of the techniques used by 'professional rebels' to resist change, she stresses the importance of listening to those who have legitimate doubts about certain initiatives. Such people are, she points out, the most troublesome 'to the conscience as well as the intellect'. Her account emphasizes the importance of creating a culture which can facilitate change through, for example, abolishing redundant committees and creating more flexible task groups which cut across traditional hierarchies.

Her account raises three particular points which are taken up in different ways by other contributors. The first of these is the nature of her vision and own personal commitment to the changes which she is pursuing. This particularly comes through in relation to her analysis of seeking to encourage wider participation in her institution from different sections of society. The second issue is one of strategy. She points out that the strongest argument in convincing colleagues of the desirability of certain changes is to demonstrate to them the beneficial implications for students – thus, the staff she brought to meet with 15-year-olds in schools in disadvantaged areas became some of the most ardent workers in relation to widening access when they saw these young people were demonstrably bright, curious and committed. In addressing the question of the culture of universities and colleges and their methods of operation, Christine King focuses on a third important topic raised in other chapters concerning gender issues and management and leadership styles. She highlights the importance which informal support networks can play for women in leadership positions, where they are still substantially under-represented.

From this broad overview we move on to three cases which, in very different ways, focus on the nature of change at the level of one of the key units in any institution – the department or division. In the first account, David Thorley reflects on the strategies which he adopted in seeking to enhance research activity. He does this through two case studies which elaborate on the difficult balance, discussed in Chapter 1, between satisfying the desire of academics to pursue their scholarly activity and the increasing requirement to use resources effectively. In seeking to persuade colleagues of the benefits of collective working – in order to develop a stronger and more focused research profile for the division overall – one of the keys to the achievement of a successful outcome in the face of some scepticism lay in his ability to persuade his colleagues that he had their best interests at heart.

He contrasts the successful outcome of his first case study with the less than successful outcome of the second. Once again, the overall objective of the change was to seek ways of improving research activity through closer co-ordination of eight research centres within his school. Valuable lessons are highlighted about the difficulties of roles which do not have visible lines of accountability, which are temporary, where the context makes it difficult to build up close interpersonal relationships and develop trust, and where the cultures are quite different. But perhaps most importantly, he reflects on the fact that he himself was not as convinced of the absolute value of the change as he had been in the first example. Richard Taylor's account describes in a graphic way the difficult choices which face heads of department as they seek to promote the interests of their own department in the light of institutional changes and other external pressures. As the university as a whole became more committed to widening access, it was not always easy to see where the best interests of his department lay. Was there a danger that it could lose its particular identity if it became too involved in 'mainstream' university activities? Or was this the best means to survival and expansion? The transformation of full-time academic staff with a background and an identity in a wide range of disciplines into continuing education specialists, required the adoption of a range of strategies. One of the critical issues he raises is the tension experienced by many in his position between the demands of the internal management of the department (and the importance of being 'seen to be around') and the necessity to spend time proactively pursuing the department's interests in the university and more generally in the external world.

The crucial step on the road to major change was making the strategic decision that the department's future lay in closer involvement in areas such as the development of a part-time undergraduate degree, the creation of a university access office, and the development of closer links with local colleges of further education. However, the actual task of managing the transformation implied by these major new areas of activity carried large-scale staff development implications. In striving to achieve the best for his department, Taylor echoes the concerns expressed in many of the other contributions about the need to continuously reflect on the extent to which change is being introduced for reasons of survival, on a somewhat opportunistic basis, as opposed to change to which the individual is personally committed.

From these reflections on general issues of implementing change at a departmental level, Peter Slee's contribution focuses on the experience of utilizing one particular strategy for the implementation of change – total quality management

(TQM). Faced with cutbacks in funding, changes of function and increasing competition he chose to utilize a TQM approach in order to facilitate far-reaching change across his department. His experience was that, far from appearing to come from 'an alien culture of industry', the philosophy underpinning TQM was in tune with the implicit values already current in his department – in particular, the emphasis on continuous improvement, a recognition that almost everyone wants to do their job to the best of their ability, and that most of the failings are systemic rather than human. In describing the process of utilizing a TQM approach, the emphasis on team working is striking. Like other contributors he stresses the value of teams which cut across traditional hierarchies and functional boundaries. This account particularly draws attention to the fact that very few, if any, activities and processes which take place in higher education are 'self-contained': all are part of a greater integrated whole. Change in one part therefore has repercussions which ripple across others with varying degrees of strength.

Following these reflections of managers in three particular departments, Jennifer Tann provides a comprehensive overview of the common issues and problems identified by heads of departments in seeking to grapple with change. This contribution is based upon the author's personal experiences as a head of department and her extensive involvement in staff development and consultancy in support of the management role undertaken by academics, in particular, heads of departments. She highlights the problems arising from lack of clarity about the traditional role of the head of an academic department where elected positions on a short-term basis, without any clear job description, have not been uncommon in certain parts of the system. Few heads of departments had the opportunity for formal training to prepare for the role, and have had to acquire management and leadership skills along the way. Amongst the eight burning issues which she identifies for heads of departments is the problem of maintaining staff motivation and morale as they find themselves up against what appears to be endless change. While at one level heads of department appear to be crying out for assistance in grappling with this type of issue, she also points to some cultural differences which arise between different academic areas. Her experience suggests that there can be some resistance to staff development from those heads who are essentially task-oriented and can be somewhat hostile to contemporary process-based management training techniques.

Chapter 2

Making it Happen – Reflections on a Varied Career

Christine King

The first problem for all of us, men and women, is not to learn, but to unlearn (Gloria Steinem).

INTRODUCTION

Only one thing is certain for those of us in the business of providing post-16 education and that is that change is a constant. Everyone who works in the field of post-compulsory education, in a university or a college, whether as a teacher, researcher, manager or administrator, is part of that change, like it or not. If I had to identify one lesson I have learnt, at some personal cost, in my career within higher education, it would be that change is a process which involves the heart as well as the head.

Some changes are imposed as a result of government policy or funding decisions and have to be implemented and managed; others are initiated internally and represent ways of exploiting external political circumstances to the institution's best advantage. A few arise from the educational conviction of individuals, usually at the top and these affect the style and direction of an institution.

I start this personal view of managing change, therefore, with some reflections on the process I have experienced during a number of years leading an academic department, faculties in two very different institutions and as a pro-vice-chancellor with specific institutional portfolios as well as membership of the senior executive team. I have learnt that to initiate and lead change it is necessary to see clearly where you want to be and feel passionately about getting there. It is also essential to be capable of taking colleagues with you. A manager of change has to be personally convinced of the benefits of the changed direction and happy that the costs are, in his or her judgement, worth paying. Nothing has been harder for me than to work out the plan, find some fellow advocates and then have to modify my views and my timetable as I meet the overly-conservative, the frightened and those who have legitimate and reasonable doubts which deserve honest consideration. The latter are, not surprisingly, most troublesome to the conscience as well as the intellect.

One result is that visions as well as plans sometimes have to be revisited and you have to acknowledge that you are wrong and that the plan will not work, or is not appropriate for the institution or for this particular time. On other occasions it will be necessary to hold firm and to set about the task of convincing others. Occasionally, and rarely, it will be necessary to forge ahead even without this support. Deciding which is the right step and how to take it is the key skill, in my experience, of leadership. It always takes much longer than one expects to implement changes and a great deal longer before their results are seen and recognized. By that time it is probably appropriate to review, restructure or reformulate policy in this area again.

There are real personal costs and it is important to be aware of these. Like many other teachers/researchers turned managers, I have had to face losses; of students, of sabbaticals, of 'serious' research and of a large cohort of colleagues. Pursuit of my 'subject' has become my hobby. The benefits are that it is possible to effect change on a much wider scale than before and that I can introduce what I believe are real benefits for the work of students and teachers. Not everyone wants to do this job, but most academics believe they could do a better job given half the chance. If I add that I am a member of that still rare breed, the female senior manager, and that this presents its own issues, it may be apparent that my experience over the past few years has been interesting, challenging and not always comfortable; it has been and remains above all, a learning experience.

FIRST EXPERIENCES

I came to senior management strong, as I thought, on vision but not, as I see in retrospect, quite so good at listening to my critics. My first attempt to introduce radical change was, nevertheless, largely successful. I led a group of good but undervalued and rather dispirited staff into a position where their talents were very publicly recognized and their future assured. I 'fought their corner' with the tenacity of a terrier and worked within the group to establish, identify and develop a 'culture' by which we worked. This was at a time when their particular area of expertise was less than popular, subject to all sorts of prejudice and financially at risk. On the whole, I think it was right to be this unbending advocate; the group flourished and continues to flourish long after I had moved on.

The potentially hostile national context required this single-mindedness. I was, I suspect, something of a problem to my superiors, unbending in defence of my team and unwilling to sacrifice anything of their interests to the greater institutional good. On the other hand, the group itself undertook a number of activities outside of their teaching and research which served the institution well in terms of profile and even income. Because some members of the group were so energetic and able, it was possible for me to demonstrate in a number of forums that its continued existence and its growth was good news for the institution. While I would now do things a little more subtlely, I would aim for the same result. What I learned, however, was what it feels like to be the leader/advocate and how hard it is to focus, from that ideological position, on the wider institutional needs or the realities of external pressures. It would have taken a lot of time and information to help me through to a more balanced view. I try, and sometimes fail, to remember this when I am aiming to move someone who is standing where I stood then to a position where they will put the institution first.

THE NEXT STAGE

Running a faculty means being Janus-faced and this may easily be interpreted as being 'two-faced'. You stand between senior management and staff and students. You act as advocate for your area but now know enough about top-level decisions and external pressures to realize that the choices are not easy. You are responsible not only for communicating decisions which you may not agree with but have 'signed up' for. Above all, you have to make change work, often in a great deal of detail.

The position can be uncomfortable and involve what, in a previous role, I would have rejected as compromise. Here communication with staff about changes is critical. It is essential, on occasions, to explain in great detail the basis on which corporate decisions have been made and to avoid the trap of simply blaming the senior management. Some of this will go on, as indeed senior management will in turn blame the government or the funding bodies, but too much of it and the manager loses respect from both sides.

Faculties often have large numbers of staff and where the small team can absorb one person who does not contribute fully, or is ineffective in aspects of their job, the problem in the larger group can be multiplied to a degree where it is visible and has to be tackled. I have learnt, at a cost, that it is best to do this sooner rather than later. Such staff, if the manager is not careful, can be seen as anti-heroes, as victims of the changes that are happening around them and which we are responsible for implementing. They are indeed often characterized by their reference to some non-existent 'golden age' when, as I was once told, 'we were citizens of this institution, not employees'. Part of the problem is that in many of us there is the closet belief that perhaps there is a grain of truth in this and thus we feel marginally guilty about dealing with those staff determined to block change in any form.

Problems like this can therefore escalate so that either the discontented are using public platforms to voice their Luddite philosophies or they keep their heads down to such a degree that overworked colleagues feel a sense of unfairness. That there has been a national move towards 'managerialism', new staff contracts and pay schemes highlights and complicates the situation. It is difficult to keep the balance between a proper discussion and sympathy for staff worries about new practices and a need to use the new tools to help bring about change. Here, as elsewhere, I have learnt that measured honesty is the best policy. While the language in which changes in contracts or pay schemes are explained has to be carefully balanced, and union and other negotiation sensitively undertaken, when the crunch comes the new measures will be introduced and it is best to work quickly to ensure cooperation and understanding. As on so many issues, lack of information means that misinformation will circulate.

Amongst the most serious and important changes which can happen at this level, is the changing of the culture of everyday work. This can include negotiated rules around meetings and memos so that trust and communication replace a display of 'rules' and hierarchies. It can include changes in the style of working and the language used, in the context of equal opportunities and the celebration of people's differences. If the culture is right and most people accept its premises and practices, very interesting things can happen. Asking members of a meeting to review its past year's minutes and decide if its role is important enough for it to continue to exist can be a fascinating experience.

I have learnt, however, that it is not necessarily conservatism that leads some people to wish to retain what is demonstrably outmoded, it is that the meeting provides a platform for their voice. In changing structures and systems to produce a more streamlined and efficient institution, it is important to find out what purpose the outmoded systems used to serve and to decide which remain legitimate needs that have to be met in some other way. There are two dangers; one is that this need will be ignored in the cause of 'efficiency' and the other is that there will be lip-service paid to democracy and the experienced and noisy will dominate and intimidate those who are willing to consider and who could benefit from changes in the way things are done.

RESTRUCTURING

Sometimes it is years since anyone looked carefully at a set of organizational structures to see if they still work effectively. Sometimes what appears to work may militate against newly articulated values, like equality of opportunity or non-hierarchical team working. In such cases there may be a need for restructuring. Short of the threat of redundancies, reorganization, especially if it involves changes in accommodation arrangements, gives most people the most amount of concern. Restructuring, especially in a context where staff roles are likely to be changed, can provide uncomfortable evidence that senior managers do have power, when the crunch comes. The resistance is often more to that uncomfortable fact than to the process itself.

Effective restructuring needs to be properly negotiated and this makes the process a long and complex one. It is, however, a mistake, in my view, to try to shorten this stage, although circumstances will vary with institutions. Here, as in other projects which bring about radical change, it is important for the manager to find champions of the new cause. The crude purchasing of support with promises of promotion (or even a particular office space) happens, of course, but is best avoided because of its transparency all round.

Here, as in other circumstances, it has been my experience that involving all staff – teaching, clerical, administrative, technical as well as switchboard and other support staff – right from the start and on an equal basis, can be controversial, but is important to the end success. Achieving structural, cultural or indeed any kind of change, requires that people work together in teams and are ready to cut through hierarchies, whether of status or role. At best, they need to be empowered to think the unthinkable. If the radical ideas come from the 'bottom' rather than the 'top', tremendous results can follow. Thus mixed teams of teachers and administrators, where every person is playing an equal part, is fully briefed and shares in the results and the sense of achievement, can, I have found, do more to change working cultures than management 'away days' or formal and regular meetings. Indeed, one of the management concepts which is used effectively in bringing about the process of change is that of the project team. For such a team, a feeling of involvement, contact with others outside the usual working group and a sense of ownership are all important.

Increasingly the pressure for public accountability which universities and colleges have been facing is being used to challenge all sorts of once sacrosanct practices. In the setting up of task groups, for example, to determine the input to an institution's strategic plan, or to determine if communication systems are working effectively, new ways of working are possible. Thus, instead of setting up groups by subject, by teaching or administrative function, it is possible to build teams which slice through hierarchies and functions. In such a mixed group, little can be taken for granted; language has to be explained and sacred icons can be and often are challenged.

I have learnt that the tougher the pressures from outside, whether political or financial, the more important it is to be transparent and honest in the making and communicating of decisions. Provided the professional rebels referred to above have learnt that they will not be tolerated should they try to silence others with their bullying, most people, given the information and a chance to respond will accept reasonable decisions made by senior management and help to make them work. People who work in education, particularly as teachers and researchers, can be amongst the most challenging to manage not least because they are trained to query every statement. Properly involved, I believe that most will use these skills to the institution's best end. Nowhere is this more apparent than when the concern is directly related to students. That students and their welfare should represent the focus of the university or college is the one point on which all colleagues will normally agree.

WIDENING PARTICIPATION

I have, this far, shared some very personal views and experiences about the management and initiation of change in my role as a departmental and then as a faculty head. I move now to a case study of institutional change. My aim here was to see changes in the constitution of the student population by encouraging wider participation from different sections of society. As part of that process I was also keen to encourage university colleagues to work more closely with further education colleges and schools and to begin to view post-16 education as one process instead of something which had a clear cut-off point at 18. By implication this also involved us deciding to reject any tendency to construct for ourselves an 'ivory tower'; a temptation we might just face as we were about to change title from polytechnic to university.

I was surprised and delighted at the honest and open discussion which met these developments in certain circles. In practice, many people within the institution were already committed to playing a central role in the region and to an informed view of the educational process. Some were school or college governors, others had children at local schools or colleges. It was an important first step to use the experience and commitment of these people to tackle the prejudices of the few who felt that contact with further education was 'not appropriate for a university' and the legitimate questions of the many about what this might mean for the future. Although the climate was not hostile, major changes were involved and a campaign to manage these was necessary.

The story starts with a personal conviction that one of the major tasks of a university is, through the education of its students, to promote social and cultural change on a national and even international scale. Together with this passion to see all groups in society represented fairly in the education system, I was fortunate enough to find myself working for a vice-chancellor who is supportive of my aims, honest in his advice and committed to educational values. I learnt from him that the soapbox I had carried around with me, just in case, since the days when I had fought single mindedly and noisily for my department, was not the right tool for this place and this time.

Thus I addressed myself first to two sets of circumstances and researched them speedily but carefully before I made any moves. One was the national agenda and what would politically be acceptable, and the other was the beliefs, values and language used by the people I would have to bring with me if I wanted to see change on the scale I looked for.

My agenda was clear. I wanted to see students from groups currently under-represented at my own and many other institutions viewing, for the first time, the university as somewhere both relevant to their lives and at which they could expect to earn a place. This included local school-leavers who would be the first generation in their family to stay on into further and higher education. Many of these live in an area with one of the lowest staying-on rates post-16 in England and where raising aspirations is an urgent need. There were already mature returners in the university and a successful access course for those without formal entry qualifications, but we needed to increase these numbers considerably by widening the network of access courses. In terms of gender, some areas were predominantly male, in line with national trends, and this needed to be addressed. My aim was to ensure that opportunities were offered to people from these and other groups at no cost, indeed at an enhancement, to the quality of experience of all students.

There were already people doing excellent work in small groups throughout the institution on different areas of what was then called 'continuing education'. There were a number of potential further education colleges and schools in the area with whom useful contact could be made, but these institutions had experienced a mixture of friendly overtures from some and a response of detachment from others.

Throughout the institution, as with many others, there was a feeling of suspicion about the process, a worry that these changes would bring about a decline in standards and that, relatively newly established as a degree providing institution, we would 'slip back' into being 'further education' if we had too much contact or too many non-traditional students. My earlier experience had taught me that most of these views were sincerely held and while I did not agree with their conclusions, I shared the aims of those who wished to ensure the highest quality of experience for all our students. It was just that we differed on what this 'quality' might constitute.

While dealing with those who saw this as a great chance to grind a stock-pile of irrelevant axes, I did my best to use the institutional language, at that time lengthy debate and detailed memos, to make my case. I was frequently close to despair at the time and energy this took from the 'real business' but here the wisdom and experience of my vice-chancellor taught me that this was a persuasion job worth doing. To my surprise it was and the hardest lesson to remember at this stage of my campaign was that sharp comments and seeming temporary public defeats often resulted in a couple of more critical converts to the cause.

It was hard also, and I sometimes failed, to ensure that those who had been working quietly for years behind the scenes did not feel displaced by my up-front approach. I was fortunate; these were strong people, committed to getting results and delighted to welcome a champion. My next aim, alongside the advocacy of the cause and the formal acceptance of policies, was to add significantly to the number of people working or willing to work in schools and colleges to help establish links.

An important factor in this stage of the campaign was that government policy was promoting the widening of opportunity and the participation of school-leavers in higher education. While there was little or no money to encourage this move, the educational arguments, together with the political imperative, gradually helped to persuade more and more people.

The best agents of persuasion were always the students themselves. On one occasion I gathered a group of teaching staff, some of them very sceptical about the appropriateness of our setting-up special compacts with local schools, to join in a visit to one such school to talk with groups of 15-year-olds. Many years ago, I taught on the 'Popular culture' summer school for the Open University. As part of the programme we took bus loads of mature students to the seaside at Blackpool to observe patterns of leisure. They got on the bus in very much the mood that the staff set off for the school visit: grudgingly curious but ready to be unconvinced. The result was the same. My 'Popular culture' students, who had never before been to Blackpool and who had sat in silence all the way there, came back wearing 'kiss me quick' hats, carrying rock and were total converts to the Blackpool way of holidaying. After the sessions with the students, my staff came back converted. These were kids from areas of deprivation; they did not expect to get to university, many did not know what a university was. Yet, they were demonstrably bright, curious and committed. In fact, they displayed all those characteristics admissions tutors regularly seek in traditional A-level applicants. The staff who came on that visit became some of the most ardent workers in the area of access.

The next stage involved building a mixed team of full-time administrators to work with academic staff on a number of defined and specific schemes. These included compact schemes, the building of a large access network with regional further education colleges, the buying and use of a bright red trailer which was taken out to supermarket car parks and agricultural shows alike, as well as a drop-in 'HE Shop' on university premises. Again, the university was fortunate to attract a young, fairly junior but quite outstanding team who began to shift mountains.

Worries about the possible negative implications for 'quality' grew less as the first cohorts of students began to pass through the system with great degrees of success, either absolute, in terms of the degree classifications, or relative in terms of the added value between where they started out and where they ended up.

There was some national publicity when the next stage of the plan was launched via a big scheme to attract students from the locality. While the trend in England is that many students, especially mature students, are increasingly considering, for financial reasons, going to their local university, it is still perceived as desirable that a student goes away from home to study. Central government is in the process of cutting the amount of student grants so the public perception of what is desirable is increasingly in conflict with the reality. Thus we were accused of doing the government's job for them, in encouraging students to stay at home and there were a few people who said, 'I told you so'. Yet recruitment numbers rose; the overall profile continued to hit a better balance and there was no sign of things being worse, just different.

It was at this time that all the work that had been done in building or rebuilding relationships with regional colleges began to demonstrate benefits that were recognized within the university. Always, deliberately, cautious in the amount of work it shared with local further education colleges, the university was able to recruit, via its partner colleges, students on to courses where recruitment was difficult. In the locality we now had a number of influential friends who knew our work for the region and celebrated this as contributing to regional development. Some funding followed these contacts as well as some profitable business and consultancy links.

As a cap on numbers, financial constraints and new research funding opportunities confront us, the challenge will be to move the drive to access into its next phase and embed it so firmly that, whatever the political climate, it is part of the university's 'mission' as well as its mission statement. I believe we are there but that the next phase must be managed. Change, as we know, is constant.

CONCLUSIONS

The more experienced I get, the less sure I am of the next step and the more willing I am to consider different ways of achieving the same ends. That may represent maturation or it may represent a healthy (or otherwise) cynicism. I like to think it represents an improved grasp of the possible, although some of the changes I have brought about in the past I would not have dared attempt if I had known then what I know now!

After 20 or so years of teaching, I have found the necessary separation of the manager, at times, quite trying. I am also clear that my experience is somewhat different because I am a woman in this position and in this attempt to describe what I wish I had known when I started, I would be less than honest if I did not comment on this aspect of my experience.

We are all different, of course, as people and as managers. Yet I firmly believe that men and women, because of their upbringing, do think and speak and operate in ways that are different, with some notable exceptions, from each other. My experience would suggest that women managers are sometimes more comfortable with change than many of their male colleagues, for example. Women know that changes which challenge hierarchies or turn worlds upside-down usually benefit 'outsiders'. I have tried and continue to try to encourage female staff, to ensure that they have information and that their voice is heard. I have not done this through having formal responsibility for equal opportunities, but in other ways. I am clear that networking with other senior female colleagues, outside whichever institution I am working in, has been the basis of my retained sanity.

This area is the subject of a chapter (or more) in itself. Perhaps what is most relevant here is the fact that I tried to find methods to support women in the institution and help them progress in their careers in a way which would suit the culture. Thus I helped set up, again, with some first-class staff who have achieved tremendous results, the Professional Women's Development Network (PWDN). The network, now run by a small team, achieves the aim of supporting women staff via a mentoring scheme and a number of other initiatives, some formal, many informal. It therefore fulfils part of the university's mission. What makes it so successful is that it scores on other points too. It earns a considerable amount of money in training contracts and grants and it gains excellent publicity for the university. The very title 'professional' allays fears of feminism. Where once I would have rushed in, I have learnt to use the political in the cause of change.

Each situation is different and the change agent needs flexible and powerful antennae to read the predominant language and cultural norms. Even if it is these very norms that are to be challenged, it is there, at least for me, that the story begins. One also needs a great deal of luck and the ability to find and keep good people to make the change happen. They are the real agents of change. In the areas I have discussed here, these people are part of a wide network which reaches well beyond the university's walls in colleges, schools, amongst unemployed women attending the PWDN courses, or chief executives attending the monthly Network meetings. The magic ingredient, however, remains the university staff, particularly, for me, those who make things happen with little money and little reward but for whom every new contact and every access student entering the university is a success. I used to send cards, buy flowers and chocolates and champagne. Now there are too many victories to celebrate, so it must be time to prepare for the next set of changes.

Chapter 3

A Learning Curve in Change Management

David Thorley

INTRODUCTION

My theme here is a description of my earliest sorties into change management. The two examples I have chosen are fairly small-scale and are, inevitably, fairly specific to the context of the institution in which I work and to my own personality and background. Nevertheless, given that first steps are probably the hardest I feel that this story could be useful to others who are at the beginning of their own journeys into change management, so I offer this personal story in the hope that others can perhaps draw some parallels, or even inspirations, from it.

The institution in which I work is a technologically-biased plate glass university which received its Royal Charter in 1966. It now has a relatively traditional academic culture, with an emphasis on research and a management style which tends towards administration rather than proactive leadership, thus leaving individual academics to develop autonomously and thereby progress – or not – as the case may be. In my own case, I have progressed via the traditional route from lecturer to senior lecturer, reader, professor, deputy dean and now head of department.

My background, however, is relatively untraditional for an academic; hence the role models that inform my actions and strategies, both consciously and unconsciously, are not the usual ones for academia. I do not come from an academic tradition. Having left school at 16 I followed craft and student apprenticeships in the automobile and electricity power industries. Both before and after I graduated I was in positions of managerial responsibility in industry. Latterly, this included the supervision of teams of engineers and technicians as well as a responsibility for activities where wrong decisions could have caused serious injury or cost lives.

This early experience has been very influential in my later career. My other main source of influence has been the senior managers with whom I have worked, beginning with my father, who was general and sales manager of a large engineering company, to superintendents and senior engineers in electricity generating stations and later, though to a lesser extent, those in my academic career.[1] I have been lucky in that virtually all of these managers have been concerned about people. They have been people of integrity, with a human side to them.

With this background, and the recognition that the people side of management was at least as important as the mechanisms, I began my own career as a change manager.

The two case studies which follow are both concerned with the need to reconcile the desire of academics to pursue their legitimate scholarly activities with the increasing requirement to use resources efficiently. This introduces the necessity for collaboration and leads to the development of distinct departmental and institutional cultures and identities, eg, to be more businesslike and commercially oriented. My earlier career and experiences were to have a considerable influence on my own aims and my strategies for achieving them.

It may be worth noting that it seems more common now for academic posts to be filled by candidates bringing experience of the world outside higher education into the academic community to the benefit, I believe, of both. This helps bridge the culture gap between academia and the world outside and I have a strongly held view that, in the case of engineering, our students should have the opportunity to be educated by practising engineers.

In the first example, I describe how I believe I succeeded in harnessing the activities and enthusiasms of a group of individuals pursuing their own goals to create a coherent group identity at the same time as significantly enhancing the individual careers of my colleagues. The second example, which followed the first chronologically, was an attempt to do the same sort of thing with a different group of people. In my estimation it was not as successful as the first, so the main purpose of this chapter is to describe both exercises and reflect on why I think it was successful in one situation and not in the other.

CASE 1: THE CREATION OF A RESEARCH CENTRE – A SUCCESS STORY

It was 1983 and, under the prevailing educational axe, the department in which I was based was being 'downsized' from around 46 academic staff to about 23. Preferential early retirement was encouraged and, organizationally, six academic divisions had recently been replaced by three, each with a new 'leader', of whom I was one. All the academic staff had been invited to join whichever one of the new groups they wished, and we three new leaders were intentionally chosen to be of such an age that we would have to live with the consequences of our decisions!

My new division consisted of nine academic staff and represented about one third of the department. It was based on a natural amalgamation of two of the previous groups, but we were joined by a colleague who had transferred from another group. Another followed later.

There was a perceived need, both within the university in general and in our department in particular, to increase the level of research activity, while at the same time maintaining the quality of our teaching and other activities. However, in engineering we did not then have much research activity so we were not endowed with many renowned and successful research professors – whatever was to be done, had to be done by ourselves.

As an inducement, the university had adopted a policy whereby successful research groups could be accorded the title 'research centre' and enjoy certain benefits. The term 'successful' meant that a certain level of regular grant income, typically £100,000 per annum, could be demonstrated, that there was a healthy throughput of research students working towards higher degrees and a steady stream of publications was appearing in reputable journals. The principal benefit was financial, and twofold. On the one hand, preferential treatment was given to members of research centres in the annual bids for equipment funds distributed within the university for supporting research. On the other, insofar as overhead income was generated on some research contracts, 50 per cent of this was returned to the research centres that earned it to reinvest in research-related activity.

Given the prevailing pressures on higher education, I felt that the key to our survival lay in establishing ourselves as a recognized research centre, and this became my goal. I was driven by instinct as much as by anything else, but believed that if we could acquire an element of financial autonomy we would have more freedom of action and some control over our own destiny.

The only two research centres that already existed in the university were quite small, highly focused and each based around a single individual. At that time, my team were, academically speaking, a pretty motley bunch. Furthermore, being self-propelled, each of us was ploughing our own furrow. It was also the case that our 'research' activities extended across a spectrum from advanced 'blue skies' work to 'applications', while the new member of the group really did no research at all – then! However, I felt that the variety of our skills and aptitudes could be turned to advantage if I could carry the others with me. Their skills were assets that could be marketed and exploited.

As engineers and applied scientists I also felt that we had an opportunity, perhaps even a responsibility, to broaden our income base. We were far too dependent financially on central government, so if we could diversify our income base we were likely to be more secure as a department. Furthermore, if we were still practising engineers we would also be improving our own employment prospects externally should the need arise; a realistic approach, given the climate at that time in higher education.

I knew I could argue that the grants, contracts and consultancy income we generated between us amounted to around the critical £100,000, but it was built up from a wide range of seemingly disparate projects. This was not surprising since promotion in academia was, and still is, based essentially on demonstrated excellence in one's own field. In the absence of a long-established research tradition, most of us had pulled ourselves up the research ladder by our own bootstraps and further promotion appeared to depend on each of us individually; or did it?

I am naturally cautious and reserved. I prefer to develop my ideas and strategy carefully, so to start laying some groundwork, I canvassed the notion of forming a research centre among various colleagues on an individual basis. Colleagues I was closest to were willing to give it a try, perhaps to humour me; one or two were a little ambivalent, but I thought that on balance more were in favour than not.

We held a meeting to discuss the proposal and I succeeded in getting agreement, but it was hard work. Two colleagues nearer the blue skies end of the research spectrum were extremely sceptical. Reservations centred on questions such as, did we need another layer of bureaucracy, would they need my approval for their projects, could we not get access to research funds independently, how would group public relations help, why was it going to be better to present ourselves as working in, say, three principal areas rather than nine, and so on.

Perhaps it helped having been a second-hand car salesman before I became an academic, but I succeeded in getting agreement that we seek recognition as a university research centre, though I had to concede that it should be open to review after one year. Never mind, it was a step in my direction – I would just have to prove it was the right way forward.

Suffice it to say that ten years later we had one of the most successful of the eight research centres within the school of engineering alone. Furthermore, not only was I awarded a readership and then a personal chair, but so too were a couple of my colleagues who had the greatest reservations about the venture in the first place. They are now among my strongest supporters and I have recently appointed one as co-director. We have a very strong research base, a healthy portfolio of research grants and contracts and have moved into some new and highly advanced research fields. How was this achieved and what lessons may be learned?

I believe one of the key features to our success was that I persuaded my colleagues that I had their best interests at heart. Certainly I had my own personal agenda, but that included helping my colleagues achieve their own goals. Having set myself up as the 'general and sales manager', I wanted them to succeed; I saw it as part of my responsibility as head of the division. Part of this stems from my belief that their success would reflect credit on my management ability even, or perhaps especially, if they ultimately go higher up the academic tree than I do. My success would lie in their achievements.

I also argued, and we all soon demonstrated, that two or three people working together produced far more than when working as individuals. There was still scope for individualism, but the foci of our activities could be complementary. In fact I was convinced they had to be. We could still lay claim, individually, to new ideas and concepts, but why not coordinate them so that they contribute to a larger whole?

In some ways my role was that of facilitator, with an eye for spotting opportunities where we could exploit the various talents that, between us, we possessed. For example, as mentioned above, the new member of the group had no prior research experience. He had joined us from another academic area in which he had been discouraged from doing any research, but was keen to join in. I was concerned that there may be a problem of self-confidence in finding himself alongside colleagues with several research contracts and long lists of publications. The task I set myself, therefore, was how to identify and harness the talents and aptitudes I believed he possessed. These included being a very sound, broadly-based engineer with a good grasp of fundamental principles, and having his feet firmly on the ground. I felt too it would be unfair to encourage him into any of the mature fields: it had to be something he could specialize in with no real competition.

I then had a stroke of luck! Out of the blue I was contacted by a former student, now in industry, who knew of our reputation for being open-minded, flexible, willing to look at almost any sort of investigation we felt we were qualified to tackle. The problem he presented was quite novel and there were no real experts already in the field. Its resolution would require a mixture of sound engineering judgement, common sense, a logical mind and the need to devise and execute some appropriate experiments. If the answers we provided were faulty the consequences could have been a spectacular display of death and destruction. Quite a challenge.

With just the minimum of encouragement my colleague rose to this challenge and he is now, some few years later, the world expert generating his own research income. It was a very pleasurable experience for me to hear him address an international audience, in London, on his work. The audience included lawyers and attorneys, flown in specially from Europe and the United States, and he now has a unique place in his own branch of our research. This illustrates, incidentally, that engineering design and research is not just about solving equations and getting numerical answers, but exercising judgement and taking major decisions. Will this equipment or that pipeline system, be reliable and safe? Are people's lives likely to be at risk?

Returning to the others in the group, and the matter of a many-furrowed field, one target was to reduce the number of furrows. This has been achieved in various ways including ongoing discussion, a recognition that research funding is susceptible to what is currently fashionable, that some topics become 'mature' subjects and classed as R&D, and so on. Before too long, more and more successes occurred where two or three colleagues were collaborating. We produced a brochure that we could all use, and presented ourselves to the outside world as a lively and versatile group, with our various activities linked to just a few key themes. Our versatility proved to be a key strength in itself, enabling us to move into interdisciplinary research fields and capitalize on new funding opportunities.

During this period, annual appraisal of academic staff was introduced and this became another trigger for discussing with each of my colleagues how their future careers may best be served. Two or three research topics have now been consciously discontinued and others strengthened, partly by having two to four people collaborating and partly by becoming interdisciplinary. For example, the modelling of complex fluid flows now embraces not only traditional topics such as pipe systems and heat exchangers but blood flow through heart valves and in the aorta, body fluids moving through muscle tissue, air flow in infected lungs and fish locomotion – all externally funded.

As a leader and manager of change in this context, I do believe I needed academic credibility, but did not need to be superior to my colleagues. In fact, I would go so far as to say that it would have been disastrous if I had pretended to be. I did not have the largest research grants, nor the longest list of publications – but I had a respectable list. I learnt later that one reason I gained support and respect from my colleagues was that I did not expect my name to be on all publications and research grants as, on occasions, happened elsewhere. It became recognized that I was pushing my colleagues to improve their positions; all I insisted upon was that they gave their affiliation as the research centre.

Among the contributions I do believe I brought to the group were a perception of the broader view, an ability to work with people and gain their trust, a little bit of 'business sense', an awareness of the need, and perhaps even a little flair, for publicizing our work, and a willingness to handle the necessary administrative tasks that the average academic finds such a chore. Thus I was often able, for example, to find little sources of money for helping colleagues attend conferences, buy a personal computer or a piece of equipment. Incidentals perhaps when taken individually, but all helping provide support and encouragement. Periodically, we also had social functions, a Christmas or summer garden party, another facet of team-building and strengthening group loyalties. These events included partners and spouses and were often held in my home.

Looking back on this period, and knowing what I know now, I do not think I would have done anything much differently. I believe the principal factors which influenced our progress included my own conviction about where I was trying to get to, and my success in gaining the trust and support of my colleagues. I had a vision of a thriving research group, but with a flexibility to respond to new opportunities built into it. I was also operating in an extremely benign environment in that targets and objectives were not set for me by senior management; I was free to set my own. There were some minimum administrative requirements associated with the broader aspects of heading an academic division, but beyond that I was left to chase my own particular rainbow and was fortunate enough to have a group of colleagues who were willing to join me. Within the university I know it is regarded as a very successful venture. Credit was given to me for the initiative in setting it up, forging a team spirit and managing the research centre. It was given to all of us for working together to make it a success.

Among the personal outcomes has been the satisfaction of seeing colleagues in whom I believed gaining recognition and just reward, including two personal chairs in addition to my own. I also benefited from experiential learning in the area of leading and managing change.

Most academics receive little or no formal training for senior managerial posts. I am fortunate in having grown up in a business environment and then spending seven or eight years in industry. This more recent experience has further reinforced my instinct that people rather than systems are the key to success in achieving goals. It has also prompted me to support my own professional development by selective attendance on management development programmes.

Another outcome was that I was appointed one of two deputy deans in the school of engineering and, more recently, head of the department of mechanical engineering and aeronautics. My role as deputy dean carried with it a special responsibility for reinforcing and integrating research in the school, a post that lasted for just under two years until a new dean was appointed and the management strategy changed. These two years proved to be a very challenging period and was, in my opinion, of only limited success. I will first describe it and then discuss reasons for why I was not successful in achieving the targets for which I was aiming.

CASE 2: COORDINATING RESEARCH ACTIVITY IN THE SCHOOL – NOT A SUCCESS

The stated task was to seek ways of improving our research activity, but there was also another agenda. It was the early 1990s and we were in the throes of yet another attempt at improving efficiency in higher education which, in plain English, meant increasing income and/or cutting costs. We in the school of engineering were regarded as having too many staff, both academic and support, funded from central resources. It was essential therefore that we recoup some of the costs from our own activities.

By now the school possessed eight research centres as a consequence of the initiatives outlined above, and these were seen as potential sources of income to help bridge the gap. Although we had other potential income streams, such as short courses and consultancy, the turnover from research activities was of the order of £1m and far exceeded all the rest. On paper, it appeared that we were generating a healthy surplus.

I perceived my task as being a repeat of the team-building I had achieved with my own research centre, so that we could focus on common aims and identify a suitable strategy, but at a school rather than at a 'local' level.

At this time we had no common forum for discussions on purely research-related issues. Each research centre was autonomous, operating as a self-contained entity, a business within a business. Like mine, all the other research centres had evolved independently; most were highly focused and did not perceive any particular need for closer association. Any proposed change was often seen as a threat to that independence and surplus funds were jealously guarded. We, the research centres, had earned them; we felt the money was ours and there was even resentment in some quarters that only 50 per cent was returned to us.

I had a lot of sympathy with this view; after all, I was still director of my own research centre, but perhaps because it was never anywhere near as focused as the others; I was seeing much broader horizons – I was thinking in 'school' terms. It is a feature of my own career development that having achieved something on one level I have an urge to move on to the next. It also meant that in some respects I became a poacher turned gamekeeper. Having previously been fairly creative myself in ensuring that I recovered and retained control of as much of the overhead and surplus income as I could for my own research centre, I was now cast in the role of persuading my fellow research centre directors to give some up into a central pot. Due to pressures being exerted from above this became the first priority; coordinating our research activities became relegated to second place.

During these two years only a little progress was made. We formed a research committee comprising the directors of the various research centres to debate the relevant issues. One tangible outcome has been that one colleague has set up and maintained a programme of lunch-time seminars to increase awareness across the school of the wide range of research activities being undertaken. I endeavoured to devise a research policy, with a set of aims, to which we could all subscribe. By making it fairly general we inched towards, and finally achieved, agreement. The next stage was to develop a strategy in order to work towards achieving these aims.

We had numerous meetings and discussions. I set up and led school-wide seminars on interdisciplinary themes where I had identified colleagues apparently working in related areas, to try to stimulate new groups. Most of these ideas ran into the sand. On the financial front, I encountered steady resistance and procrastination despite trying to tease out ways of ensuring representation in all decision-making on how pooled resources would be utilized. Two years on I really had very little to show other than an ongoing programme of seminars, some publicity material which brought together a review of all the important research activities in the school, and a greater personal awareness of colleagues and their activities. In the event, this has proved to be useful much later.

What, on reflection, was going wrong; what were the problems; why was I not having the success that I sought? I think part of the underlying problem was that I had great difficulty in focusing on a clear all-encompassing goal in which I could believe myself. At the time I could not visualize what the end result could be in terms of something to which I could feel committed or had ownership. No wonder, really, that I could not sell it!

In retrospect, I also feel that there were too many independent spirits that I was seeking to influence at the same time – an example of the adage that managing academics is akin to herding cats. The breadth of activity was far greater than across my own research centre. This in itself should not have been a problem, but I could not at that time get a broad enough view to see an interconnecting whole. I also had difficulties in relating to researchers who believed their own work ranked above all other activities and some who even expected 'the university' to provide them with all the facilities they felt they needed. Cultural differences on the balance between teaching and research, and a stubborn blindness to the economic realities of our position, were much greater than I had anticipated.

Another facet was that I was now working at a different level of interpersonal relationships. In my own research centre I was dealing with colleagues who had grown accustomed to the way I ticked and who were willing to be led. In starting things up I had taken the initiative so we could create our own business. Here, I was dealing with other entrepreneurial directors of research centres who had done the same thing. Individually, we had gained quite a lot of autonomy but now I was perceived, not without some justification, as seeking to clip our collective wings, curtail some of the freedoms.

In my role as divisional head and director of a research centre I benefited from being in a position that carried responsibility and accountability. I was in a clearly understood and accepted line management position. Here, I was on an equal footing among colleagues who had all pulled ourselves up from the common pool. Although a deputy dean, I was not, at that stage, a head of department. I had no real seniority or even a visible line of accountability to give me any leverage; everything had to be achieved through discussion and mutual agreement. It was a manifestation of democracy (or academic freedom!) at its most stagnant.

An added drawback was that my position was known to be temporary. The post of dean would shortly be vacant and there was no clear view of the future. This reinforced my ambivalence. Also, why should we directors of the research centres apparently give up either funds or autonomy in an environment where salary scales are virtually flat? As professors we were about as far up the academic tree as most of us were ever likely to get. We had built up an activity in which we each had considerable freedom of action, a considerable amount of job satisfaction and, at times, the opportunity to augment our salaries.

But here we have also encountered one of the management conundrums of modern higher education, namely: to whom or what are academics accountable, to whom or what are we committed, how should we be rewarded? We have commitments to our students, to our profession as educators and to the profession associated with our own subjects. Where we seem to have a lower priority is a commitment to the university as a corporate body.

CONCLUDING REMARKS

In comparing the two scenarios described above two or three key issues stand out. These may be perceived as tensions between the often conflicting demands on us as educators, as researchers and scholars, and as administrators. My own experience points to a rapidly changing culture within the academic scene as it moves from a relatively elite environment to a mass higher education system. The pressures for accountability, quality and efficiency being imposed on the senior management are feeding down into the system, challenging the traditional autonomy and freedom of the individual academic and scholar. No longer can we plough our furrows in splendid isolation and expect, as a matter of course, to be left alone. On the other hand, this does not mean that career aspirations cannot still be fulfilled!

In seeking to introduce change there has to be vision, a goal to be worked towards. It has to be expressed in a way that people can buy into, can share ownership of, and can feel its relevance and importance to them for their own career development. As managers in education we should be sensitive to the insecurity that change can bring and work towards demonstrating that versatility, the ability to change, is actually a strength, a quality in itself. The cultivation of this should be one of the objectives of the appraisal system.

Comparison of the two cases also suggests that where clear lines of responsibility and accountability exist the authority that accompanies them is respected, especially when it is demonstrated that the responsibility extends both upwards and downwards. As an engineer with an industrial bent, working among engineering academics, I am probably fortunate since these concepts are not seen as particularly threatening as they are well-recognized in our profession. One of the challenges in academia is to combine the benefits of teamwork, which requires an organizational structure and its attendant sets of rules, with those derived from the freedoms and relative independence normally associated with a university environment.

I commented earlier that most academics receive little, if any, formal training in management skills, including managing their own personal effectiveness. I find it very useful to occasionally take time out to reflect on the goals I am seeking and my strategies. Even relatively simple things like a review of personal time management need servicing periodically. Too many of us also do routine tasks that can be dealt with just as effectively by our support staff, releasing time to us for more productive academic work while at the same time making the jobs of our support staff more enjoyable and interesting.

We are now in an age when we cannot avoid having to plan for the unpredictable in higher education. However, we do have the skills and the opportunities to survive. To do this we need to operate within some broad framework to give a sense of stability and continuity, but this does not inhibit the scope to be creative, flexible and versatile. Therein will lie our future success.

POSTSCRIPT

Although at the time I became very frustrated and even a little disheartened with the second case described above, I ultimately realized that negative experiences can also be a source of learning and knowledge. Following my appointment as head of department and the arrival of a new dean, the information and contacts I had made during the seemingly abortive two years as deputy dean became very useful. Our new dean joined us from a highly regarded company and at an operational level we have a new management strategy. The executive committees are small, there are clear lines of responsibility and authority, and goals and expectations are more clearly defined. Not only am I much more comfortable with this personally, but we are actually achieving many of the things we set out to do just two years previously.

NOTES

1. I have drawn little on conventional management material, but publications I have found useful include:

Adair, J (1988) *Effective Time Management,* London: Pan

Brown, H and Sommerlad, E (1992) 'Staff development in higher education – towards the learning organisation', *Higher Education Quarterly,* 46, 2

Office of Public Management (1992) *Managing Fundamental Change: Shaping New Purposes and Roles in Public Services – Proceedings of a One-Day Conference,* London: Office of Public Management.

Chapter 4

Accessibility and Institutional Change

Richard Taylor

INTRODUCTION

Over the last ten years the pace of change, and its fundamental nature, within higher education has been unprecedented. This has become a commonplace but it is important to assert at the outset of any analysis at the micro level because the ubiquitous climate of change obviously provides the critical context: none of the established practices within higher education can be taken for granted any longer and, more importantly, none of the cultural assumptions about higher education and its purposes and practices can be assumed to be permanent.

This context of continual change has been especially noticeable in some of the older universities, and perhaps particularly so at the University of Leeds, which has undergone rapid and radical transformations in the last few years.

My intention in this chapter is to reflect upon these series of changes from the perspective of a middle manager in one area of the university's activity – continuing education – which has been centrally involved in some of the key aspects of these changes.

THE DEPARTMENT OF ADULT CONTINUING EDUCATION AND THE UNIVERSITY OF LEEDS

The department is one of the largest of its kind in the UK: we have 24 academic staff, four and a half administrators, 12 clerical staff, and 12 research contract staff. In addition, we employ around 200 part-time tutors each year. The annual turnover is just under £2m p.a. The department was founded in 1946 and has undergone numerous reorganizations since. We have responsibility for continuing education across a large region, encompassing West Yorkshire, most of North Yorkshire and part of Teesside. More than 10,000 part-time adult students enrol with the department each year.

The university is committed to the development of continuing education as an integral part of its mission. Overall, there are over 30,000 continuing education students involved in university programmes and this is set to increase rapidly over the next few years. In addition to my department, there is a small department of continuing professional education and a unit within the school of education for the development of continuing education research.

My own involvement in the department and the university began in 1970 and it may be useful to describe my roles briefly in order to contextualize the ensuing discussion of management practice. I graduated in politics, philosophy and economics in 1967 and then spent three years at Lancaster University as an administrative assistant. In 1970 I was appointed to a similar post in the department at Leeds, responsible for organizing the liberal adult education programme. I translated to the academic staff in 1973 and was appointed warden of the university's centre for adult education in Bradford, a post I held for ten years. During this time, in addition to successful liberal adult education provision, we developed a strong community education programme, and a range of partnership arrangements for both provision and action-research with the statutory and voluntary sectors in Bradford. I moved back to Leeds in 1983, was appointed senior lecturer and, with others, created the department's Pioneer Work programme of work with unemployed people and other disadvantaged groups. I became director of extramural courses in 1986 and, after a university reorganization of continuing education, head of department in 1988. I was appointed to the chair of adult continuing education in 1991.

At the most general level, the last ten years has seen the department move, in the context of the university, from a marginal to a central role. To explain this and identify the nature of this shift, some examination of changes in the wider university is necessary. As noted earlier, the notion of accessibility is the key to this linkage. But to appreciate how this fits with the university's overall development this too needs putting in context.

Leeds has been a large and traditional civic university, committed both to the full range of high quality undergraduate and postgraduate teaching, and even more to research across the whole range of academic areas. In the late 1980s the decision was taken to expand student numbers very rapidly. Simultaneously, a new modular structure, involving over 3,000 individual modules, was introduced for all undergraduate and postgraduate programmes over 1993 and 1994. A centralized timetable has been introduced and a two-semester system also began in 1993. Student numbers have increased from c.10,000 full-time equivalents (FTE) in 1988 to 17,000 FTE in 1993, making Leeds one of the largest single universities in the United Kingdom in terms of full-time equivalent students.

Within this overall expansion, there has been an explicit commitment to broadening the base of the student intake. The most recent Corporate Plan, for example, states that the university has

> *an obligation to be more responsive to under-represented groups ... we have steadily increased our level of activity ... and now have much more effective procedures for widening access. The new Access Office will 'foster and carry forward our initiatives to widening access, ... expand the range of liaison activities ... and serve as a one-stop information point ...' (p.21).*

As a large and research-intensive university, Leeds has a national and international role. But it also has a very strong regional identity. Obviously, my focus is on continuing education, but there are other equally important aspects of this regional focus. To take just two examples: the university's medical faculty provides a major network of contacts in the region. Similarly, the university is one of the largest validating bodies in the United Kingdom and it has 'affiliate' arrangements with a large number of colleges in the region, ranging from the 'colleges of the university' through to colleges of health and further education colleges.

Many of the initiatives in the university relating to accessibility have been linked to continuing education, broadly defined. One of the decisions I took, in discussion with colleagues in the department, was to involve myself, as head of department, in as many of these *university* developments as possible. I discuss below three case study examples. Here, it is relevant to outline the pros and cons of this approach. On the negative side, there are obvious costs to the department: more and more of my time is spent on university work in these various areas which is, at best, of only indirect benefit to the department. Moreover, once such initiatives are begun they inevitably lead to other areas even more tangential to continuing education interests *per se*. In turn, this often leads to my involving colleagues in the department in university activity which has no direct, immediate bearing on our work. There are also problems in the context of managing the department: the more time spent away from direct involvement in departmental issues of programming, curriculum development and so on, the more remote a head of department becomes from academic and other staff. While this can be coped with on a number of levels – ensuring a structure whereby there is regular individual contact with all staff, having informal social relationships, 'being around' as much as possible – these are nevertheless real problems.

However, in my view, the positive advantages far outweigh the difficulties. Continuing education is inherently an innovative and change-driven area and it is essential for success that the organization is able to respond to, and where possible initiate and steer, change. Again, continuing education is inherently multifaceted as well as multidisciplinary. We have therefore needed to be involved in a wide range of institutional developments to try to ensure that continuing education makes its contribution to the common weal but also that continuing education is networked into new developments. Activity of this type automatically involves me and, by extension, various groups of colleagues in the department, with a variety of separate networks and groups across the institution, often producing benefits of cooperation over continuing education which were not planned but resulted from the initial personal contact.

Overall, this policy has worked well. The department is now better known, better understood and better regarded than in the past. And we are involved in a range of university-wide developments. However, cause and effect are hard to identify: the university was moving in these general directions anyway and much of the progress is due to this and to a highly supportive senior management. The most that can be claimed is that the policy of involvement in the centre of the university has helped these processes.

CHANGES IN THE DEPARTMENT AND IN THE UNIVERSITY

There have been two categories of fundamental change and development for the department over the last decade, and particularly the last five years. First, there has been a transformation in full-time academic staff roles; second, the department has responded to changes in the university's policy and practice and seized opportunities wherever possible to play a leading role. One effect of both these changes, especially the latter, has been to bring the department and its work more into the mainstream of university activity and development.

The change in staff roles has been both fundamental and complex and has required – and still requires – a great deal of managerial time and ingenuity. In large continuing education departments like mine, most staff come originally as subject specialists rather than 'continuing education professionals'. In the 'old days', the role was one of teaching adults your specialism, with appropriately designed curriculum and pedagogy, and (in some cases) undertaking research in your specialist field. When continuing education departments were separate, 'extramural' organizations – in effect mini-universities in their own right – this was an appropriate structure. But it is wholly inappropriate in the current context. Staff need to become continuing education specialists in terms of both provision and research. In terms of provision, this means being programme managers and initiators, working closely with external agencies and colleagues across the university and also acting as quality assurance and line managers for the large numbers of part-time tutors involved in continuing education delivery. In terms of research, this involves matching original subject expertise to research activity in continuing education *per se*.

These changes are essential if a continuing education department is to have a credible and legitimate identity, and if continuing education work is to achieve and maintain a high quality. But, managerially, they are difficult developments to handle. Understandably, staff are loyal to and identify with their original subject disciplines and they are resistant to yet more 'administration'. Continuing education research, too, is a contentious area: many colleagues are keen to maintain and develop their subject research and, equally, reluctant to develop continuing education research areas. Managerially, my view has been that it would be highly counter-productive to try to force the issue on the research question. We have tried to create a supportive, facilitative environment for continuing education research through the creation of a research and postgraduate unit with an experienced and senior continuing education person devoting half her time to this work. The department also devotes a lot of time to staff development programmes, including the continuing education research area. Finally, as head of department, I talk regularly on a formal basis to all full-time staff about their work profiles and this always includes a discussion of their actual or potential development of continuing education-related research. I should add that, in my view, subject-based research should not be actively discouraged. This again would be counter-productive; and much excellent research work has been produced over the years from within the 'extramural tradition'. There is anyway an argument for maintaining research activity in at least those subject areas where the continuing education department is a major provider at degree level. My line has therefore been to be flexible, to ride both horses in terms of research but nevertheless to stress the particular importance of continuing education research and to indicate clearly that in the long term this must have priority.

The position over continuing education research is thus complicated. On professional *provision* roles, however, I think the position is clearer. Given the size of the continuing education operation, the diversity of work involved across a large and varied area, and the importance of cost-effective and quality assured administration and delivery, there is little room in the department for full-time academic staff who 'only teach'. Even here, though, I think that flexibility and sensitivity have to be shown. There are some colleagues who are best suited to a 'teaching only' role, and this is usually linked also to a subject-based research profile. This is acceptable managerially, in my view, as long as this is restricted to very few staff and as long as at least a proportion of their teaching takes place in innovative areas.

This whole process, which has transformed the department, has involved considerable collective and individual staff development. As in other management contexts, in universities and outside, this transition could only be accomplished by consensus and collective but flexible advance: managerial dictats would not have produced the desired result!

Despite tensions and uneven development, the transition has been accomplished well. Two contextual factors have been particularly important. The first has been the supportive attitude and practice of the university's management and administration, and the consequent expansion of the department and its work; and the second has been the relatively positive national framework for continuing education since the mid-1980s – following a very difficult period in the last years of the then Department of Education and Science's involvement in continuing education funding and policy, and the general retrenchment in universities in the early 1980s. Both of these factors have enabled me to manage change positively, with an agenda of growth rather than contraction, and within an atmosphere of staff development rather than defensiveness.

This is an appropriate stage to introduce another variable: how far is it professionally sensible to become involved in national continuing education policy contexts? Again, after consultation with colleagues, I decided it was in the department's and the university's interests for me, as head of department, to devote a significant amount of time to involvement in the national body for continuing education, the Universities Association for Continuing Education (UACE). We also decided that similar involvement of other colleagues in this and related continuing education work, both in the UK and overseas, should be a similarly high priority. I estimate that I spend the equivalent of around one day per week on UACE work, and that departmental colleagues in total devote a further day to UACE or associated bodies. There are obvious costs here, but the benefits, though intangible, are considerable: a high profile for 'Leeds continuing education', an involvement in policy-making and funding issues for continuing education not only in UACE but also in the Higher Education Funding Council for England and other national bodies, and a series of networking relationships.

All of this sounds – and has been – very positive. But there are negative aspects too. The university system, and the whole educational system come to that, has been the victim since the early 1980s of persistent cutbacks. There has also been not only rapid change but a lack of any strategic direction by government. This is not the place to labour these points but it is important to note the effects of this general, unhappy, situation upon continuing education. For example, the recent freezing of student numbers in universities, following previous strong encouragement to develop access programmes, and the continuing growth of the further education sector, has led to real problems both for individual adult students and for continuing education departments such as my own which have several successful access courses in humanities, social studies and science.

Another macro problem has been the persistent and simplistic emphasis by government upon training and vocational education as being the only viable form of access (and at times, it seems, of further and higher education in general). I have taken the view that the correct response to this is to work with 'their' agenda to try to achieve as much of 'our' agenda as possible. Whether this is the correct line to pursue is debatable – tactically, politically and practically (the dangers of incorporation in this context are returned to in the final section of this chapter). Nevertheless, I think that this somewhat opportunistic managerial policy is justifiable in the current difficult, volatile climate. The danger is, of course, that the underlying objectives and rationale become marginalized, even forgotten, in the entrepreneurial rush to climb on the endless procession of (funded) bandwagons. This is a personal risk, so to speak, for the manager concerned: but it is even more of a risk for those working within the organization who are necessarily less involved in the strategic thinking involved.

CASE STUDIES

1. Developing part-time undergraduate degrees

There are also negative as well as positive aspects of the three case studies of my involvement in institutional and departmental change. The first of these is the development of part-time undergraduate degrees. Like most of the large civic universities but unlike most of the 'new' universities, Leeds had virtually no tradition of part-time degree provision for adult students. In recent years there have always been significant numbers of part-time taught masters students, many of them from overseas, but the undergraduate programmes have been composed overwhelmingly of full-time, standard age and nationally-recruited students.

In the mid-1980s Leeds began an initiative to develop part-time degree provision and I was asked by the university to assist the two senior members of staff involved (professors of physics and geography respectively) in formulating proposals and taking them forward. How far should this initiative have been centred in my department and how far should it have been a university-wide initiative? My initial gut reaction was to try to establish this as a department-led exercise; in retrospect I realize that this was mistaken. If part-time degree development were to take off and become a significant part of the institution then it had to involve, from the outset, several departments and, long-term, virtually all. It would have been fatal for it to have been seen merely as an extension of my department's activities. We could not have resourced adequately a full-scale part-time degree programme. More importantly, part-time degrees could not have become a mainstream activity.

I was persuaded out of my blinkered 'departmental' approach at an early stage – by wiser counsels! But I had a related managerial problem in my own department. Why should we become involved at all, my colleagues asked? This was a diversion from non-award-bearing liberal adult education, would incorporate us into other departments' curricula and practices, and we would anyway be acting primarily as a recruiting agency for other departments' student cohorts. Moreover, the costs, in terms of staff time for development and administrative support, are high. This has been a persistent theme through the eight years or so of (rapid) part-time degree development. With all the other pressures on staff in my department, this is understandable. However, I am convinced that for both principled and practical reasons we have to be centrally involved in this development. This policy has the general support of colleagues and this department is by far the largest single contributor to what is now a sizeable university programme. However, there are still misgivings and these represent a genuine dilemma. How far should my department's energies be devoted to providing the resource-intensive basis for a university-wide development which, in the long-term, will be of benefit largely to others in the institution (as well as, of course, to the community at large)? Would it not be better for us to devote ourselves to providing a high quality, innovative *departmental* programme? This presents sharply the dilemma of 'mainstreaming' continuing education. If we initiate such work which then becomes the property of the university and its specialist departments at large, then what is our long-term role?

This involves structural as well as managerial and staff issues. My view has been that we have a triple role as far as teaching delivery is concerned: to act as innovator and catalyst for new institutional developments in continuing education, broadly defined; to ensure curriculum development and pedagogic practice appropriate to adult and other non-standard background students; *and* to play a central role in at least some of the areas of direct provision in which we have academic strength. In all these ways, therefore, we have been involved in all the major purpose-designed part-time degree schemes so far developed: humanities, combined social studies and local and regional history. The costs have been high, however. For the first two years of operation the department was not funded for this work: the university was still working out a system for financing us over and above our continuing education grant. Admittedly the numbers involved were small but the overall income forfeited was significant; and the amount of scarce full-time staff time expended on developmental work, curriculum planning and liaison within and outside the university, was very considerable – and the opportunity costs high.

I have been keen nevertheless to have a strong presence not only in the teaching and development of part-time degrees but also within the university office established to coordinate and develop the work. The various posts in this office have been filled largely by secondment and I have tried, successfully, to ensure that departmental colleagues were placed in these positions wherever possible.

Overall, then, the managerial strategy here has been to encourage departmental involvement in part-time degree development almost irrespective of cost – either direct financial cost or opportunity cost. This has been essentially an *a priori,* strategic decision, taken on the grounds primarily that we cannot afford not to be involved in such work, and that it will lead to enhanced credibility and networking in the university and may also, incidentally, produce financial gain. To some extent this is a leap of faith: in my judgement universities are going to become far more reliant on locally-based, part-time students and we have to be in there making the best use of both our local knowledge and our pedagogic expertise.

However, it is also part of a policy of 'dispersal': that is, of creating a multifaceted department which responds flexibly to new needs and opportunities. I have based this policy on several factors: partly my judgement of political realities where no single stream of funding seems secure in the long-term and it is therefore sensible to spread risk and not have all the eggs in one basket; partly because this development fits clearly and centrally with the university's and the department's access mission; partly to enable networking across several areas to create strategic alliances which can be used for other developments and, in hard times, can also be called on, hopefully, for political support; and partly, to be honest, a personal disposition for variety and diversity in professional life!

Nevertheless there have been problems. There are real costs in terms of scarce staff time, lack of adequate financial reward, and serious doubts about the cost-effectiveness of this work compared with other continuing education provision. Politically, there have to be doubts also about building up an alternative and explicitly mainstreamed structure for an expanding market which could compete directly with accredited continuing education provision.

2. Creating a university access office

The second case study – my involvement in the creation of a university access office – relates closely to the part-time degree development. Until 1993, the university had no single contact point for the student enquirer and no single focal point for access development. There was my department, the undergraduate admissions office, the schools liaison office and so on, but no real coordination. With the university's general commitment to both access and increased recruitment of standard age and background students, this could not continue. Several attempts were made to create an appropriate structure for both policy and staff development. A loose grouping, the 'Wider Access and Review of Courses' (WARC) group laid the foundations, and in 1992 the university agreed to the establishment of an access office. The group that prepared this proposal consisted of the pro-vice-chancellor for teaching, the two deputy registrars, and me. The general aims of the office were agreed as follows:

- to present the university in the most attractive and effective ways possible to its existing constituencies for recruitment onto its undergraduate programmes;
- to coordinate existing functions in the university in the access area (including schools and further education liaison, and some aspects of the admissions process);
- to liaise with local and regional bodies concerned with access and guidance issues;

- to act as the university's focal point for developing a more accessible institution and to concentrate upon particular initiatives to achieve this aim (for example, the development of a credit accumulation and transfer scheme);
- to devise methods of promoting the university and its provision to new constituencies of potential undergraduate students from the United Kingdom and other European Union countries, concentrating upon particular target groups;
- to collect and disseminate programme and other relevant information concerning the university to these constituencies.

There were positive and negative sides to my involvement in this process. The most important single argument in favour of supporting this initiative was of course that access was integral to the mission of the department and of the university, and that this office was an important element in taking forward the whole concept and practice of accessibility. There was also the point that *some* kind of coordinated structure was bound to emerge and it is always better to be 'inside the tent...'etc. There were also potential advantages for the department in coordinating our access roles with those of the wider university.

The same difficulties applied, generally, as in the case of part-time degree development. But the managerial roles in the access office proved complicated. Should I, or some other departmental colleague, become director of the office, responsible for policy, budget, staff and so on? Or should this be the responsibility of the registrar or indeed another academic 'bought in' by the university on secondment? Or should a new post be advertised? In the event, a compromise emerged whereby the office became the responsibility of one of the deputy registrars in terms of line management and budget, and I became responsible for 'policy'. Whether this is a satisfactory structure remains to be seen. Certainly, some of my colleagues are not entirely happy with it. Apart from organizational complexity and lack of clarity, there are persistent worries about overlap and confusion between the department and the access office.

In the context of this discussion, the details here are unimportant. But what it does illustrate is the continuing problem of the proper demarcation between the centre and periphery, between institutional and departmental functions. This dilemma applies to *all* university structures and of course the 'new' universities have a far more centralized managerial structure than the 'old', where there is still a fair degree of departmental autonomy. Interestingly, this is reinforced by the 'resource centring' system which devolves budgets and therefore a large degree of decision-making power to departments. This runs counter to the more general tendencies within universities towards increasing managerialism and central direction. However, leaving these wider concerns on one side, it is clear that the structural tensions (not personal ones, I hasten to add!) between the centre and the departments apply with particular force to continuing education, and are part of the whole question of whether or not continuing education should be fully 'mainstreamed' rather than being the primary responsibility of a single department.

3. Developing collaborative links with local colleges

The third case study is rather different. In 1991 the university decided to take a more proactive stance in its discussions with further education colleges. There were various reasons for this, partly to do with the changing status of further education under incorporation, but largely related to the university's policy shift to become far more involved than hitherto with its own locality and region. I was asked to take responsibility for the development of a university strategy for continuing education partnerships, centring on franchising of level O (equivalent to access to higher education level) and level 1 (equivalent to first-year undergraduate level) provision but including a wide variety of mutually beneficial development – access pathways and specific access arrangements, validation, joint project development, joint staff development, credit accumulation transfer scheme, and so on.

Given the national context of government squeeze on arts and social studies numbers, and the drive towards science and a generalized vocationalism, it was clear from the outset that the bulk of this work would be in science and engineering areas. Overall, this has worked quite well and partnership arrangements are now in place or under discussion involving 14 regional further education colleges and some 20 or so university departments.

The managerial tasks here have been quite complex, partly because the matrix is inherently complicated with so many different players with different cultures and agendas – in the further education colleges, but also within different departments in the university. I should add, though, that this diversity has made for a fascinating and useful series of experiences. I have been on a steep learning curve not only in relation to further education but in the context of the practices and cultures of some parts of my own institution with which I was unfamiliar.

In some ways, this further education development has had a beneficial impact on my own department. For example, our science access provision has been helped by the network contacts established with further education colleges, and our general adult education liaison and cooperation, previously with local education authorities but now, because of incorporation, largely with further education, has also been helped. Generally, though, my role here has been clearly a university rather than a departmental one. It has involved trying to manage change on a number of fronts – further education, higher education, government policy on expansion (then contraction!) and so on. But it has presented a familiar management problem: the brief is open-ended and, when there have been successes, opportunities for further development expand rapidly. How are developmental roles in further education/*university* work contained so as to allow time and energy for *continuing education* management? This is a common dilemma but it is writ large here because, on the one hand, there is a notional amount of my time paid for by the university for this work (20 per cent for this and the access office), and on the other hand an ever-expanding demand, which *has* to be met in large part if the partnerships are to thrive and prosper.

LESSONS LEARNED FROM PRACTICE

In this as in the other case study contexts there are important issues of staff development. It is a truism of all management that the most difficult aspect of the process is managing people and, within this, the hardest aspect of all is managing people through times of change and thus uncertainty and stress. A series of obvious but important points need to be made here – although obvious to state, however, solutions are by no means easy to achieve! First, a good manager has to have a strategic view of where the organization is heading in the medium term. I have tried to do this by taking the department forward as an increasingly integral part of the university's wider strategic view of growth, accessibility and quality. The difficulties here are that fundamental values, practices and cultural attributes may be distorted or even jettisoned if this process is undertaken in too opportunistic a way. Certainly, some of my colleagues feel that we have moved too far from our original mission and have become partially incorporated in an alien culture: the enterprise, market-oriented world of education in its post-Thatcherite phase. Second, the key to staff development in a climate of change is taking staff with you and ensuring that they not only *understand* change and the, sometimes regrettable, reasons for it, but that they also have a sense of *ownership* of the change process. Similarly, the experiences of change, while often exhausting and frustrating, should result ultimately in colleagues having some sense of personal professional growth and benefit. Third, staff development activities must be planned carefully and professionally: time must be set aside to enable colleagues to take part, rather than these just being 'add-ons' to an overcrowded schedule; and individual evaluation and profiling, and subsequent action to take this forward, must be built into management practice. Finally, staff development must be flexible: no homogeneous system will suit everyone, especially in such a heterogeneous and individualistic environment as a continuing education department in a university.

If these techniques can be applied successfully then change can come about consensually within a framework of strategic planning and with a clear acknowledgement of collective purpose. The borderline, in a climate of rapid change, between flexibility and participation on the one hand, and directionless drift and low morale on the other, is a narrow one. Here, as elsewhere in management, balance and sensitivity are everything!

There have been, broadly, two sets of external factors affecting my management practice, one good and the other bad. The university context has been almost wholly beneficial over the last few years. As noted earlier, the university's general mission and agenda integrate very closely with the department's and, on the professional and personal levels, relations have been constructive, helpful and facilitative. At governmental level, as everyone is aware, the context for higher education as for all other education has been very negative, to put it mildly. Not only have there been severe resource constraints, there has also been an absence of educational strategy. These problems have applied particularly to continuing education which has undergone fundamental changes in the last decade. The early 1980s were particularly difficult but we emerged, nationally, with a good continuing education system. With the ending of the binary division, the whole structure of continuing education has been reviewed and fundamental changes will be brought in over the next few years. There is no need to labour the point here, but the result has certainly been to make the management of change considerably more difficult. Had *both* external factors been negative then our position would have been well-nigh impossible. As it is, we have survived and prospered, modestly, with, I think, a reasonably high degree of professionalism and cost-effectiveness. I hope that the practice of the management perspectives outlined here have contributed something to that broadly successful development.

I turn, finally, to a brief discussion of management strategy in the wider perspective of the general ideological context. Government and universities are all in favour of access as part of the mass higher education agenda; so are professionals in continuing education, of course. So far so good. But the ideological thrust of government is almost wholly towards access as a means of instrumental and crudely vocational training. And this is within a supposedly apolitical framework which is, in fact, clearly value-laden with simplistic notions of transforming educational culture to capitalist market values and structures. I take it as axiomatic that everyone in continuing education, and virtually everyone in higher education generally, is opposed root and branch to such perspectives.

If this is the case how should we respond? Should we adopt a purist and independent approach, reaffirm our social purpose and effectively socialist culture, and have nothing to do with the mainstream? Twenty years ago I would have argued strongly for something along these lines. Perhaps I have been 'incorporated', like most of the Left, but my *professional* (though not really my *political*) views have certainly changed.

My experience has demonstrated to me that, as I noted earlier, continuing education has been able to work very effectively with other people's (government and so on) agendas to achieve at least a part of *our* agenda. Trade union education in the 1970s is one example whereby a supposedly exclusive training curriculum was used legitimately for broader liberal education purposes. The REPLAN initiatives for unemployed people's projects funded by the Department of Education and Science and the National Institute for Adult Continuing Education, were another. In fact, the whole history of continuing education since 1945 can be interpreted, in one sense, as the triumphant survival against all the odds of liberal, social-purpose adult education on quite a large scale. Despite repeated attempts to 'vocationalize' and 'professionalize' the whole provision – and culture – and bring it into conformity, it has survived.

From the managerial perspective, then, I would argue strongly that we *should* work within the mainstream, we *should* cooperate with a range of external agencies which are concerned with objectives quite different from ours, but that we should recognize that there is a need to review regularly our own perspectives, agendas and organizational culture. In my departmental context, my essential role has been to encourage and facilitate those diverse developmental initiatives within a flexible framework, and to ensure that as far as possible the staff in the department are happy with our strategic planning and with the changes we are introducing. In addition it is the manager's role to provide a clear lead on policy and a clear articulation of that policy to both the inside (the department) and the outside worlds (the university, the

Higher Education Funding Council for England, *et al*). In the end, the human resources of the collectivity of the staff are everything: unless the collective support and agreement is there, nothing else will work – especially in a context of change. That is why, ultimately, staff development is so important, and why the high quality and commitment of the continuing education staff at Leeds is the single biggest asset we have.

Chapter 5

Using Total Quality Management as a Management Tool in Educational Support Services

Peter Slee

INTRODUCTION

What follows is an account of how a team of educational managers used a total quality management (TQM) process to plan for change. But it is not a chapter about TQM. If that sounds contradictory let me explain. Stripped down to its bare essentials, TQM is simply a particular (though highly structured) approach to management. As every manager will know only too well, no one can do your managing for you. So the first task for any manger interested in TQM is one of translation, that is, applying the TQM formula to one's own management context.

This chapter is about that complex act of translation. As such it has five parts: the context which shaped the change process; our reasons for turning to TQM change management models; the planning process; implementing change; and evaluation.

CONTEXT

I was the newly appointed head of a university external relations department[1] with some 36 staff and six specialist sections:

- PR and Publicity – responsible for daily contact with media and for official university publications;
- Schools and College Liaison – responsible for coordinating student recruitment at undergraduate level;
- Careers Advisory Service – responsible for providing careers guidance to university students and for liaising with employers;
- Graphics – responsible for designing university and departmental publications. As a 'market-dependent' area required to break even on budget, Graphics tendered for private work;

- Reprographics – responsible for printing and copying most internal documents. Also tendered for external work;
- Audio-visual and Photographic Services – responsible for providing photographic services (including slide-making) and audio visual services to university staff to support their teaching and research.

I identified four major issues which needed to be tackled.

1. Doing more for less. The university was dealing with the financial pressures brought about by government policy. As a department we faced a previously agreed, but now immediate, 12 per cent cut in our budget. It seemed certain that with the drive for efficiency gains now an annual process, more cuts were in prospect. Yet consultation with my colleagues revealed that the demands on our services were increasing. We clearly needed to become focused, to ensure that we were concentrating our energies on the right things. But how?

2. Market forces. Our university was beginning to devolve budgets on a trading company model (TCM) under which our customers would be free to use external suppliers. We would no longer have a monopoly of the internal market. We would have to learn to provide an excellent service at competitive prices. In short we must not only do the right things, but learn to do them right. But how?

3. New kid in town. Every new manager needs to earn trust and commitment before embarking on a change process. But how?

4. All this and my work too? Like most managers in most institutions, everyone was busy. Making time for a major strategic planning exercise, when every colleague is weighted down with pressing business, is clearly tricky. How do we make time to plan for change in order to shape it?

CHOOSING TQM

So why did we choose TQM as a model to facilitate change? After all, the TQM concept and associated methodologies were developed in an industrial, particularly manufacturing, context.[2] There were two reasons: philosophy and methodology.

Philosophy

The TQM philosophy is simple and elegant. It comprises three interlinked elements.

1. Continuous improvement. An uncomplicated but profound notion that the only way to stay ahead of the competition is to provide a better service to customers. That means continually improving the service in ways that raise its value to your customer. As an educational support service we had few hang-ups with the concept of 'customer' or service. We had begun to recognize that structural changes in the way our organization was beginning to devolve financial responsibility opened up the prospect of competition, which in turn might threaten our position as service providers.

2. Staff want to be able to give of their best. Everyone who comes to work wants to do their jobs to the best of their ability. Clearly if colleagues want to give of their best then you will always get continuous improvement, providing you (a) allow them to do so and (b) help them to channel their energies and skills in pursuit of business objectives. We believed our biggest resource and asset were the skills we possessed.

3. Remove barriers to progress. Though people are willing to give of their best, systems usually prevent them from doing so. Indeed TQM 'guru' Joseph Juran suggests that 80 per cent of the problems and 80 per cent of the inefficiencies in any workplace are caused by poor management (Juran, 1989). Deming (1986) put it as high as 95 per cent. In short, the failings are systemic rather than human. The answer to this problem is to devolve responsibility to the lowest possible level within the organization and thereby encourage and help staff to identify the barriers to effective working. This in turn means enabling staff to participate in the setting of the business objectives and procedures that relate to their own work. As a manager I found this idea attractive. Management of others' professional skills has to be based on trust. Any professional management system must be actively participatory. In short, far from appearing to come from an alien culture, the TQM philosophy seemed to be tailor-made to our situation and skills.

Methodology

The TQM methodology is built on three basic ideas which focus everyone on the removal of the barriers to effective working.

1. Focus on process. Identify the process by which a given task is carried out. Every work process towards a given end is comprised of small steps, and every small step becomes the focus for critical analysis.

2. Create a process team. Bring together everyone involved at each stage of a given process into a team; together the members can analyse the interactions which make up the process.

3. Customers. The process team is bonded by the concept of the customer. In TQM the customer is the person at the next stage in the process. The moment you pass work to a colleague you become their supplier, and they your customer. As a supplier it is your job to provide your customer with the best possible service. The process team then work together to identify ways in which they can improve service to their customers, and thereby to eliminate the barriers to effective working.

THE PLANNING PROCESS

The TQM approach sounds seductively simple. But how does a management team get started? The answer is now, from just exactly where you are. Two things are necessary. The first is *time* for staff to get together to plan. In our situation the notion of impending crisis meant that we recognized the need to make time.

The second is *preparation*. The TQM planning process requires clarity about the objectives of your organization and clarity about one's own current work processes. This is clearly essential for a support service. If a support service is not supporting the achievement of core objectives, it has little future when the going gets tough. It is also important to take time to relate one's own work process to the objectives of the organization, and to ensure that one's own daily activities are focused on meeting defined work objectives. In a departmental, federated structure this is a line-management responsibility.

We established at departmental level our own work processes; we defined a 'process' as 'a systematic series of actions directed to the achievement of a goal'. We then agreed to establish a departmental workshop at which we would attempt to match our own work processes against institutional objectives. At the workshop we then asked three simple questions:

1. Does each of our work processes contribute to achieving a university objective? Our processes included 'produce a university prospectus', 'produce an annual report', and 'produce career destination statistics'. University objectives, derived from its strategic plan, included 'recruit more students', 'manage finance', and so on. We produced a matrix and where the process impacted on the objective, for example 'producing a university prospectus contributes to recruiting more students', we ticked the box. If not we marked it with a cross.
2. How effective are our processes (a) in absolute terms, and (b) in relation to our competitors? Score each out of 5.
3. What other work processes might we be doing to help achieve university objectives?

This exercise achieved three things. First, it gave us a very clear idea about the value of our work in the context of wider organizational objectives. There were some processes upon which considerable time was expended which had no discernible impact on any of our university's superordinate objectives. In the context of a 12 per cent budget cut we needed, and now were able, to focus more clearly on doing the *right* things.

Second, we began to get a clearer idea of how we judged our own performance. One fascinating insight was that the work processes which gained the most ticks were invariably those with which we were least satisfied, whereas those which gained high performance marks were those which had least impact on the institution's objectives. In short, we had a clearer idea of what we needed to be doing better, an invaluable lesson in the context of fierce competition for work from outside suppliers. Third, we were better able to build team consensus about our departmental mission and objectives.

The next stage was for us to begin to develop a detailed operational plan (see Figure 5.1). Having identified the relative importance of their own work processes as they had defined them, my colleagues worked with their own teams to:

- define their own operational goals, ie, what they are seeking to achieve;
- identify the processes to deliver the goals;
- analyse the sub-processes – the single actions which make up the series that define the process;
- build the work into a detailed operational plan.

The final plan took two months to develop. Once in place it showed the relationship between:

- a cohesive service-oriented mission statement;
- clearly defined objectives aligned to the mission;
- goals aligned to the objectives;
- detailed operational plans showing progress towards the goals;
- resource implications;
- evaluation methods.

What we produced was hardly earth-shattering. How could it be when so much of what we identified we were doing already? What was important, however, was that it was now overt. We could share our plans with our colleagues and our customers, and all within the framework of an institutional plan to which they too were bound.

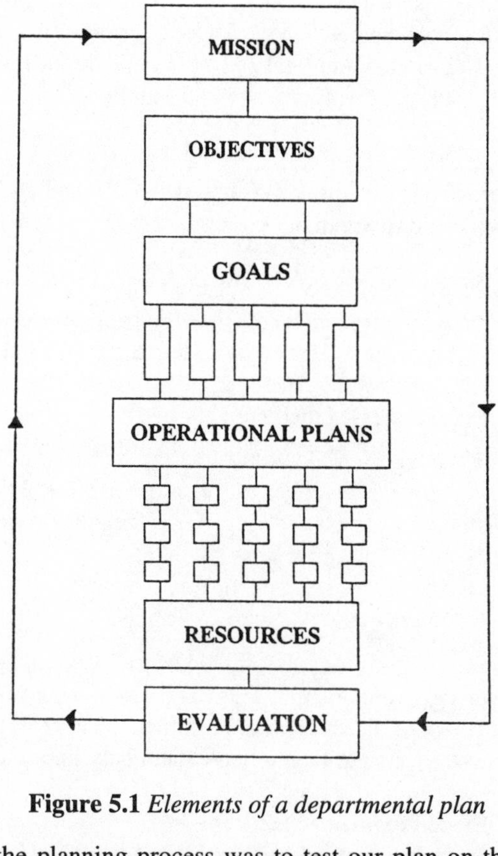

Figure 5.1 *Elements of a departmental plan*

Our final step in the planning process was to test our plan on the end-users themselves. We convened a meeting with our heads of academic and other service departments and sent them the new plan. Our meeting was a success. Our key 'end-users' were our academic colleagues. It was they we had to serve well if we were to continue to attract the resources we needed to stay in business. Our meeting with them was an important step forward in developing a new open dialogue within which we could deliver and improve our service to them. We also had the satisfaction of knowing that at least if we were not doing the right things, no one else knew it!

IMPLEMENTING CHANGE

The planning process helped us to identify what was important and how well we were performing. We now had the strength simply to abandon aspects of work which made no discernible impact on our new departmental objectives, and to focus on improving our performance in areas of greater strategic importance.

We began our new programme by taking time out to develop process planning for those work processes which we scored high in terms of strategic importance but low in terms of performance. We developed over 20 such projects in the first year. But for our purposes I will take you in detail through one project – the redesign of our postgraduate prospectus. I have chosen this one for two reasons: first, readers can, if they have a mind to, consult its successor in most libraries, and second, we made some fundamental mistakes from which we learned a great deal.

We used in broad terms the steps set out by Joseph Juran in his seminal work, *Planning for Quality* (1989). The process worked as follows.

1. *Form the planning team.* This comprised the process head (the manager with responsibility for producing the product), her two staff and me. We also invited colleagues from other sections within our department to help develop the methodology.

2. *Define the process.* We then drew up a process diagram in which we set out the key activities in stages which we believed needed to pass through to achieve our end product (Figure 5.2). This diagram helped us to determine who our customers were.

3. *Define your customers.* In TQM methodology you have two sorts of customers:

- internal customers – the person 'down the line' at the next part of the process. For instance, when you write to a colleague to request information, that colleague becomes your customer, and you their supplier. When they return the information, the process is reversed;
- the range of end-users of the product. In this case they were academic departments and their customers – the potential applicants.

TQM methodology insists that customers should be included in the planning process. Why? Because the driving force behind TQM is the provision of improved services to customers. How better to discover what customers want than to ask them? What better way to get the service right than to have them help improve it? In drawing up the process diagram we realized we had made our first mistake. We had not involved our customers. We needed to broaden the team. We pulled in new internal customers including graphic designers, printers, research managers in departments and the pro-vice-chancellor for research.

4. *Talk to your customers.* We began with our internal customers. We raised a simple question: which of your needs does the postgraduate prospectus meet? We had no ready answers. So we initiated a survey among 120 of our research students. We asked them three key questions: why they came to consider research at our university; what information they needed; and how helpful they found our publications.

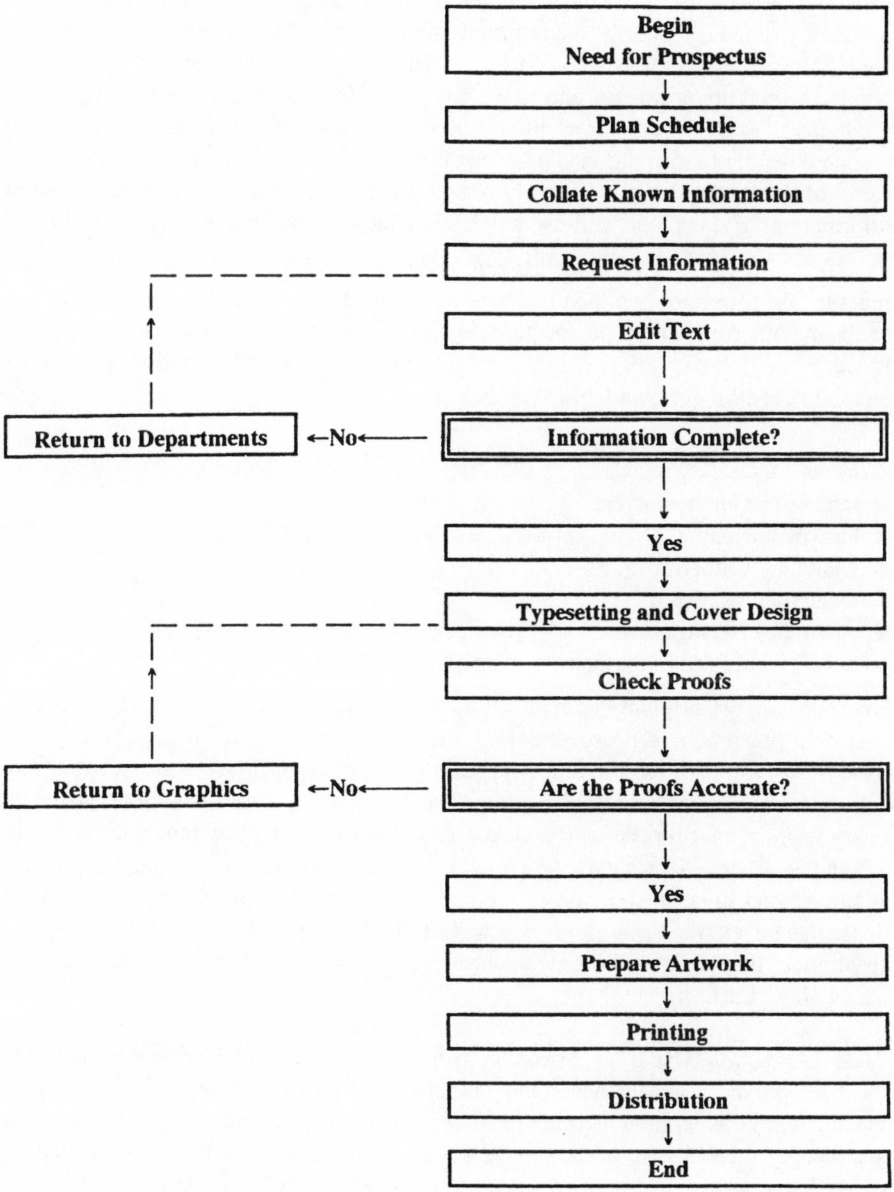

Figure 5.2 *Process diagram*

The results were enlightening. We found that most students applied to us for just two reasons: first, personal recommendation and second, in pursuit of an advertised research grant. Half simply made initial contact with a named person in a department. Almost all said they looked to the department to provide detailed information about research opportunities, and to the prospectus for a snapshot of the university as a whole. Most said our current publications were poor. Most departments had not prepared detailed information. Those that had had not done so in a helpful form. We were told our prospectus was poorly organized, old fashioned and lacking in useful information. In short, our 'end-users' were not getting what they needed.

5. *Check out the competition.* Having identified the features our own students regarded as important, we then matched our competitors' products against them. By analysing other university prospectuses against a clear set of criteria, we were able to identify 'the best of breed' against each criterion. We now had 'benchmarks' against which to develop our own work.

6. *Design the product.* We now had a clear idea of:

- who our product was for;
- how they used it;
- what they wanted from it;
- when they wanted it;
- when they would use it;
- how it would need to match up against the competition.

But more importantly we had realized our second and biggest mistake. The production of a postgraduate prospectus is a sub-process of a wider and bigger process called 'postgraduate recruitment'. As such it is inefficient to view in isolation any sub-process and treat it as free-standing. The implications of this revelation are enormous. Institutional processes run across functional lines. Unless processes are fully aligned, unintended problems will always occur across the functional boundaries. What we had done in the past was to treat our prospectus as a narrow functional departmental chore. In so doing we were failing to develop its content, form and structure to the needs of those who were going to use it. In short, it did not meet the needs of our customers.

7. *Make the leap.* Using our research information and awareness of process management we produced and launched the new product. Our new approach helped forge a much closer collaborative working relationship between the range of specialists whose knowledge and skills we needed to draw on. Our immediate customers – the departments – were also much more prepared to supply helpful and useful information.

EVALUATION

So was it a success? The answer is yes ... and no. On the positive side our customer evaluation showed that the end-users liked it and found it easy to use. They found the information they said they needed and in a form that accorded with their own selection 'process'. But, we had production problems. We ran three weeks behind deadline and some of our department customers were less than happy with the photographs in their entries. What had gone wrong?

We traced these problems to one important area – attention to detail within the process structure, and there we found our third mistake. We had not taken the TQM methodology down far enough. We needed to take each part of the process and break it down into a more detailed sub-process. For example, where photographs were concerned we asked departments to send us their pictures as part of the 'request information' stage. We simply used the pictures we were given. But our colleagues had not been able to appreciate how their photographs would look as part of the final text. The next time they saw the text was at typesetting stage when photographs had not been scanned in. They could not relate the photograph to the text.

Our response therefore was to create a separate 'box' on preparation of photographic material which included, as part of a sub-process, preparation of a detailed brief to departments on requirements, preparation of a laser proof with scanned pictures in it, and scheduled meetings in which we 'walked' the proof over for face-to-face discussion.

In short, what we learned was that without a detailed set of sub-processes around which measures of performance can be developed and analysed, it is impossible to target the root cause of persistent problems. The focus needs to be on process not product, because once the product is produced it is too late to put it right. As TQM specialists put it, to focus on the end product is like driving in your rear view mirror.

We learned from this exercise and began to translate the results into other process planning sessions. We found that once we established a robust planning structure for one generic product (a brochure) it became easier to manage other work of the same type (undergraduate prospectus, departmental brochures, annual report and so on). In 1993 (a year after I left to join my present institution) the university won awards for its undergraduate prospectus and departmental leaflets, and was commended for its annual report and postgraduate prospectus.

SUMMARY

What you have read is an account of the way a small management team in one particular university began systematically to manage its workload. The pressures we faced are common to all colleagues in higher education today. Doing more for less in the teeth of fierce competition is simply a way of life.

We adapted elements of the TQM planning procedures developed by Joseph Juran. At the functional level they worked very well. We learned to understand and build on the profound notion of the internal customer, and to recognize the importance of customer-supplier relationships. We recognized the importance of learning to adopt a more detailed focus on process, and by doing so reduced errors and the resultant re-work.

Our biggest lesson is one which has implications for every institution. It is that, at the macro level, every institutional process is 'cross-functional', that is to say, it runs across departmental boundaries. We had begun by treating our postgraduate prospectus as a self-contained process, when in truth it should have been viewed as a single sub-process in a wider institutional strategy to recruit postgraduates, a strategy which in turn should have been based on meeting perceived customer needs at each stage of their decision-making process. Such a strategy would be truly cross-functional for it would need to incorporate departmental research strategy, promotional material, customer-care systems, central and departmental admission systems, regulation changes, financial systems, accommodation and estate strategies.

The implications of market-funding have not yet made their full impact on the planning, governance and structure of traditional educational institutions. But the time is at hand. As our dependency on core funding is steadily reduced, it becomes ever more difficult to avoid the lesson that a sound corporate strategy is one which matches institutional skills to market opportunities. If we are all to become market-led institutions, then traditional administration – inward-looking, focused on functions and geared for stability – has had its day. The focus for the future must be on systemic management: the aligning of cross-functional institutional skills to customer needs – in short, on the sort of analysis for which the TQM methodology is an ideal tool.

NOTES

1. I wish to thank Marlene Clayton, director of staff development at Aston University, for her advice on TQM and critical input to this article, and Professor Sir Frederick Crawford, Vice-chancellor at Aston University for introducing me to TQM. Needless to say the shortcomings of this work are entirely my own.
2. For a helpful introduction to TQM in industrial and educational contexts, including an historical narrative of the development of TQM, see Edward Sallis, *Total Quality Management in Education* (Kogan Page, London, 1993); see also, FW Crawford, *Total Quality Management* (CVCP, London, 1991).

REFERENCES

Deming, WE (1986) *Out of the Crisis,* Cambridge: Cambridge University Press.
Juran, JJ (1989) *Planning for Quality,* London: Collier MacMillan.

Chapter 6

Managing Transformations in University Departments

Jennifer Tann

INTRODUCTION

'Change', said Disraeli, 'is inevitable. In a progressive country, change is constant'.[1] To those who have been heads of departments and schools in universities in Britain over the last ten years or so, Disraeli's comment may raise a wry smile. Change has been constant and inevitable but it may be questioned whether it has all contributed to progress in higher education. There have been instructions to expand, to maintain a steady state and, more recently, penalties for exceeding student numbers. Changes in fee levels have recently adversely affected non-clinical departments which had earlier been encouraged to recruit students funded only on a marginal basis. Research assessment has been introduced together with teaching quality assessment and staff appraisal – and, in 1993, the binary line was abolished.

Universities, through the Committee of Vice Chancellors and Principals (CVCP), have responded to and sometimes anticipated government intervention, notably with the Jarratt Report (CVCP, 1985) and Reynolds Report (CVCP, 1989) and the implementation of their recommendations. The machinery of decision-making within universities has been streamlined, strategic decisions becoming resource-driven, and academic audit has been introduced. Innovation in universities, from being more or less supply-led, located within the existing rules, easily blocked by sectional interests and generally slow, has become strategic, frequently top-down, more responsive to perceived demand, breaking out from existing rules and more generally imposed. It is the imposition of change, with what is perceived as inadequate consultation and dissemination of information, which has contributed to a sense of alienation amongst many university staff.

What follows is based on my personal experience as head of department and head of school in two older universities, followed by a period as head of school and dean of the faculty simultaneously. This chapter is also informed by research, consultancy and training within higher and, to a lesser extent, further education, where I have acted as a facilitator with groups of senior managers, heads of department and senior academics in a diverse range of institutions. I have, in addition, been a tutor for the

Northern (older) Universities Consortium for Leadership and Management Training for senior academics. These experiences have provided opportunities for mutual sharing and learning and the recognition that there is a diversity of models of internal university organization and departmental management. The experience has also shown that most people managing at the middle level in higher education experience, to a greater or lesser degree, similar tensions, frustrations and rewards. I have been privileged to hear many points of view and share many experiences while the opportunities for my own reflection and learning have been enriched.

THE ROLE OF HEADS OF DEPARTMENT

Some heads of departments,[2] particularly those who have been in the same institution for some years, experience a tension between their perception of the university or college mission and their own sense of collegial values. This tension is more likely to be pronounced in universities where heads feel that they have little direct communication with the centre. I have gathered from observation and direct report by heads from consultancy and training interventions with staff from a dozen or more universities that the proportion of time spent on the respective activities of teaching, research and departmental management by heads has changed over time.[3] Ten years ago departmental management was usually referred to as administration. Heads of departments in the older universities probably spent between 20 per cent and 30 per cent of their time on this activity. Now, heads are devoting at least 50 per cent of their time, particularly if they have a fully devolved budget to manage, in addition to responsibility for the management of other resources.

The problem for heads of departments begins with the inadequate definition of the role. This is an extension of the question posed by Mintzberg (1973) and others in the context of manufacturing – 'what do bosses do?' The majority of heads in the older universities have had to explore the boundaries of their role for themselves. A brief description of functional responsibilities of heads of departments may be found in university ordinances and when a head of department's post is advertised, some form of description of the post is available. However, this can rarely be called a job description. The difficulties reside in the inability of many schools and departments to describe the role and tasks of head on the one hand, and on the other the inability of a university to provide an agreed set of generic principles which can describe the role of any head.

The responsibilities of the head of department in many older universities are increasingly coming to resemble those of their counterparts in the former polytechnics, which traditionally advertised such appointments as part of the management structure. But while there are differences in emphasis the responsibilities of the head of department reside in three main areas. First, they include duties within the department such as responsibility for strategic academic planning, the allocation of duties to and the management of all staff, including responsibility for induction, staff development and safety; the admission, teaching and welfare of students; the management of financial and space resources as well as equipment; the promotion of academic standards in teaching and research; responsibility for implementing college or university policy on such matters as academic audit, staff appraisal and codes of practice. Second, the head is responsible for representing the interests of the department at committees and boards of the university; s/he becomes an information node communicating with the centre and receiving information from the centre which may need interpretation before being disseminated to colleagues. Third, the head of department is an academic representative of his/her field with peers in Britain and overseas; s/he plays a role in scholarly societies and peer review journals, speaking at conferences and giving seminars.

Job descriptions, where they exist, rarely contain reference to dynamic elements in the role, implying that adaptation and improvement is not expected of heads of university departments. Such an omission is notable in research and teaching as well as in departmental leadership and management. The burdens on the head of department include, on the one hand, a greater specificity of duties in relation, for instance, to people management, with no corresponding performance indicators or standards on the other. In one university with which I am familiar it is stated in the staff handbook that 'members of staff are required to carry out such administrative duties as the head assigns', while in another, heads of department 'must ensure that staff are performing their duties adequately and must deal appropriately and without delay with staff whose performance falls below standard'. The issue concerns that of the member of staff who refuses to do the assigned duties or who agrees, but simply goes through the motions. Furthermore, when mention is made of 'performance below standard' – what standard? Where is the ruling, where is the case law? It becomes a rhetorical question to ask whether heads are recruited and selected for their abilities to perform these many and varied tasks. Heads of departments were, usually, recruited to the higher education sector, particularly to the old universities, for their abilities in research and teaching. Management and leadership skills have had to be acquired along the way. The question remains to what extent staff development currently contributes to the competences of a head of department as well as how receptive heads are to management and leadership training.

TRAINING AND LEARNING

Many heads of department have had little prior experience of management training unless they have been recruited from or have had prior experience in industry or the public sector. Some universities have formed consortia for heads of departments' management training and there have been some interesting experiments. Few training needs analyses have been carried out, however, and for those who have had some involvement as facilitators in management development for heads, there has been a fairly common experience of participants seeking solutions: 'I want answers, not to be told there is no single correct one'. A number of heads of department feel uncomfortable, initially, with experiential learning on which much modern management training is based; particularly those who have a task and input orientation to their own teaching. A concern for and understanding of process is not one that is acquired at a one or two day course but, rather, is developed over a longer period.

The training and development needs of heads of departments can be assessed in a number of ways. Needs can be self-reported. These, by definition, tend to be one-off and may be a reactive response to a published course programme rather than a systematic self-appraisal of training and development needs. Many staff development managers will say that self-reporting tends to be undertaken by those who already recognize the value of training and development rather than by those who have little experience of it. In a survey of heads of departments in a college of an older university, I asked respondents to rate their level of confidence along a linear scale for 16 aspects of managing a university department. No gender stereotyping was evident in the responses on, for example, the management of financial and space resources but, overall, heads of humanities and law departments, who were more likely to be women, felt more confident on people issues than their counterparts in science and engineering. All heads felt reasonably confident in the allocation of staff duties, delegation, staff development and equal opportunities (although female heads felt more confident in equal opportunities than male). The areas in which heads felt least confident were in disciplinary proceedings and the management of conflict. There were five aspects of departmental management in which some heads were more or less equally divided in feeling confident or not, namely communication, financial management, staff promotion, negotiation and the giving of feedback to staff.[4]

The use of techniques such as repertory grids or assessment centres for the identification of training needs is almost unknown in universities although they have been practised widely in industry and other parts of the public sector. More commonly, initiative is taken by an individual senior member of staff or head of department. In my own university the vice-chancellor meets with deans and heads of school for a weekend once a year to discuss a topical issue. Development needs of heads of department can also be identified by third party observation and report. This technique is applied very little in higher education. A working party of staff development managers and senior academics may be established, for instance. But in this context there is a tendency for the outcome to appear to suggest that staff development is something that 'other people' need. It was, however, one such working party which led to the establishment of the first consortium of older universities for the purposes of training in leadership and management for senior staff.

Amongst the most important contributions to my own learning as a head of department have been the work of Beckhard and Harris (1987), Bridges (1991) and Schön (1979). I have attempted to apply Schön's insights on reflective practice to my own situation and find that running through a personal mental video of the day takes no more than five minutes. I try to note down learning points from reflecting in and on practice, warts and all, remembering the good as well as the episodes that I do not want to repeat. Beckhard and Harris remind us of the need to ask and confirm the answers to the question, 'Why change?' before proceeding to describe the future desired or to audit the present situation. Bridges' approach on responses to imposed change is a timely reminder of the fact that people internalize change at different rates, that there is a need for 'endings' before 'beginnings' can happen and that 'endings' can evoke responses similar to those in bereavement. The colleague who, incidentally, thrives on change but also remarked that he 'mourned' the loss of a programme, was making a significant point on the process of change in the department. Beginnings are imposed, but there is a difference between an imposed start and an accepted beginning and the effective change agent attempts to synchronize the two as closely as possible.

EIGHT AREAS OF CONCERN TO HEADS OF DEPARTMENT

So what seem to be the most burning issues for heads of department? In the light of my own experience as a head of school and discussions with many in a similar position, eight aspects of management in universities regularly come to the fore: succession planning and induction for heads of department; strategic planning and the involvement of colleagues in the managing of change; the reluctance of heads to initiate a departmental management team; uncertainty about the process of delegation and the negotiation of staff loading; academic staff motivation; appraisal as an aid to management; lines of communication to and from the centre and lateral communication with other heads of department in the institution; time for research. I will consider each of these in turn.

1. Induction

Across much of higher education in the UK, the appointment of a head of department may be for anything from three to five years and may be renewed. Overlap between an incoming and outgoing head is not always possible and may not be desirable when change is required. But an incoming head of department rarely has any induction to the role. Where an induction pack is provided by the personnel department it will generally contain necessary information on aspects of the contract of employment. What it usually does not contain is a clear chart of the management and decision-making processes of the university, a calendar, highlighted with the boards and committees which the head is expected to attend and may even have to chair, and the terms of reference for these boards and committees. At the departmental level a useful induction pack might contain lists of staff members, their length of service, their teaching load and research interests and productivity, together with an indication of their external professional affiliations.

I greatly appreciated the initiative of the senior administrator in sending me photographs of all the staff in my current department prior to my taking up the post. This meant that on day one I knew everybody by name. Other documents which are helpful include diagrams showing the organization of the department and its decision-making machinery; copies of procedures and codes of practice; and the most recent set of external examiners' reports, together with those of the departmental and faculty audit. Most incoming heads would appreciate some hints concerning departmental culture or 'the way we do things around here'. Is there a staff common-room? If so, is coffee-time a custom that people value? Failure to attend may quite unnecessarily raise hackles. Where do people go for lunch? Do support staff like to receive birthday cards? Is there a Christmas party? If so, what form does it take? How can the head find out when staff are available? Is there a centrally kept movements sheet recording occasions when staff are not in the department? Is there a timetable which records all people's teaching, including service teaching? The absence of this kind of information can contribute to misunderstandings which could be avoided. As one head of department recently commented, 'I learned everything on the hoof and had regular wrist-slapping from the centre when things went wrong'.

Problems for incoming heads are often located around the trivial but irritating. One new head of department arrived in the university in late September with tea-chests of books and research material to find that the retiring head (who had been presumed to have left the university in July) had not moved out of his office so that the new head's papers and books were all dumped in the corridors. Another new female head of department discovered that the nearest washroom was known as 'Henry's toilet' (but other males were permitted to use it). Another incoming head of department discovered that the new colleagues intended throwing a farewell party, to which the incomer had not been invited and was not supposed to know about, for the retiring head. The fact that the department had had all summer term and the subsequent holiday period in which to bid farewell to their retiring head seemed to have escaped them. Another incoming head, on being asked on appointment to notify the departmental administrator what his requirements were for office furniture, requested floor-to-ceiling bookcases. This was approximately five months before taking up the post. Nothing happened. The months went by and shortly before he was due to take up post, and having learned the hard way from a previous rather similar situation, said that there clearly was little point in coming until the office was ready. The threat worked and the shelves appeared on time. Another head of department discovered upon arrival that he had been referred to by anxious new colleagues as 'the vice-chancellor's Trojan horse'. Such a reception inclines a head, on a bad day, to ponder on who needs enemies when they have colleagues like this.

2. Strategic planning

It is clear that heads of department, in their responsibility for strategic planning, are expected to produce plans which contribute towards the attainment of the overall academic mission and objectives of the institution. There is evidence that perceptions of the relative tightness of the relationship between a departmental plan and that of the university or college varies with the length of service of the individual in the institution. When heads of department in one university were asked to rate on a scale from 0–100 the extent to which they believed their departmental plans should relate to that of the institution as a whole, those who had been there for more than ten years produced a mean score of 76 whereas the relative newcomers produced a mean rating of 86. This would appear to endorse the benefits of mixing heads of department from different institutions for the purposes of senior staff development, particularly for an institution where there has been relatively little staff turnover.

Heads experience different priorities and pressures depending, in part, on the academic subject. Some heads of departments of engineering or physics report the over-riding objective as being 'to get undergraduates in and increase the quality of intake', while departments with a low student-staff ratio are faced with the likelihood of having to lose staff. One older university undertook a strategic review of each faculty and department, considering its performance against equivalent faculties and departments in other universities in the region, recommending mergers of small departments and reductions in staff numbers even in departments with a good research rating and buoyant undergraduate recruitment. Some universities have a clear resource allocation model, the formula of which is widely known and which permits departments to engage in strategic planning with a clearer knowledge of likely outcomes. Heads of departments, therefore, have crucial decisions to make in terms of departmental resources in time and space as well as the allocation of financial resources for the pump-priming of specific projects. These are heavy burdens to bear if heads do not involve colleagues in the planning process. 'Just tell me what you want me to teach' is a common response of a hard-pressed lecturer who has 'become very frightened' by the pressures. Heads report that departmental colleagues are 'just overwhelmed with all the things to do' and they feel unable to spend time standing back from the day-to-day operational issues to contribute to planning for the future. A kind of desperation breaks out and phrases like, 'they always move the goalposts' and other sporting metaphors come to the fore. The equally hard-pressed head of department can thus find him or herself more or less alone in scenario-planning for the future.

3. Departmental management teams

There is sometimes a reluctance among heads to establish an advisory group which may be interpreted by colleagues as evidence of elitism, managerialism, or 'a kitchen cabinet'. The reality is that, in a fast-changing environment, the staff meeting held twice termly or so is unlikely to be an effective body for strategic planning, both on account of the infrequency of its meeting and on account of its size. Anyone who has tried to develop policy from scratch via a staff meeting will recognize the virtual impossibility of doing so. But a staff meeting can be a most effective way of helping to develop and refine proposals which have been initiated in a smaller group. Increasingly, heads of larger departments are creating advisory groups. These may consist of all senior staff or of people holding particular positions of responsibility; they may be elected by a staff meeting or selected by the head, irrespective of seniority, on the grounds of competence. The head of department who clearly distinguishes between the advisory role of such a group and the statutory decision-making body such as the departmental committee or meeting usually reduces irritation and anxiety amongst his/her colleagues.

Uneasiness about an advisory group or senior management team takes several forms. Many heads avoid the language of management at all costs so that they engage in 'managing without appearing to do so'. The head who said, 'I feel overwhelmed by the management process' spoke for many others. While in most departments certain administrative tasks such as admissions, welfare tutor, course team leader and examinations officer have been identified for a number of years, there has been a confusion over the designation of roles concerned with strategic planning with the need for rapid responses on the one hand and maximum staff involvement in the process on the other.

4. Departmental structure and delegation

The diffidence of some heads over managing and the anxiety of their colleagues about being managed may be partly underpinned by a confusion over the interpretation of departmental structures and the organization chart. It can be helpful to make a clear distinction between the lines and routes of decision-making within the department, (including a clear indication of how the decision-making lines link with those beyond the department to the faculty and committees of senate), and the lines of individual accountability. There is an understandable reluctance of heads to produce an organization chart which suggests line management relationships and yet, particularly in a larger school, the head will of necessity have to delegate major areas of responsibility to others who must be able to require the fulfilment of certain tasks by individuals. A third distinction can be made, namely that of the structure of work and the flow of tasks. Human organizations are rather better at devising additional procedures than eliminating older ones. It might be an illuminating experience for a head to become a piece of paper for a day and see what happens between a preliminary enquiry and the conditional offer of a place. And there may be conflicts of interest as, for example, if money is handled in departments where the requirements of financial audit may conflict with the desire for streamlining procedures.

Delegation, and the recognition that it involves more than asking an individual to undertake a task, is a process that a number of heads find difficult. This may be, in part, because heads themselves experience the pressures exerted by senior colleagues who require responses 'yesterday'. Most academics will recall one or more occasions on which a task has been 'delegated' at the last minute in the knowledge that it has been on a senior colleague's desk for days. Delegation can only be effective with sensitive negotiation, a clearly defined time-frame, appropriate resources, the clearing of lines of authority and an arm's length rather than parrot-on-the-shoulder relationship with the delegate, a regular checking that all is well and, most important, recognition and appreciation of a task accomplished.

Since the mid-1980s a number of university departments have been using formulae for the equitable distribution of workload to individuals. The trigger is generally the need for major strategic change. A department may be undertaking a drive to increase its research selectivity rating, and some staff may have reached near breaking point as, during a period of change, it has been easier to ask an already effective but busy person to perform an additional task rather than a low-achiever. There comes a point when resentment against those who are perceived not to be pulling their weight can begin to simmer. It is at such times that perceived equity comes to the fore. It will be recalled that most universities expect heads to deal with those whose performance is inadequate. But how? Disciplinary procedures exist but where performance indicators are imprecise and the job descriptions of staff equally so, and this will be the case for many staff appointed ten years or more ago, disciplinary procedures are not only difficult but unpleasant. There are some significant advantages to the introduction of a loading model and heads and their colleagues who have done so claim that the difficult period of negotiation and implementation was worthwhile. The loading model can help to ensure equity in loading between individuals by placing loads in the public domain. A loading model also provides a common language in which a diminishing unit of resource can be discussed in the context of a mixed departmental economy. Furthermore, a model allows the establishment of 'normal' duties so that additional duties can be noted on an 'overtime' basis, for example, evening teaching. Moreover, peer pressure can be far more effective than individual pressure exerted by a head of department.

5. Motivation

A declining unit of resource, coupled with changing demands in the marketplace, have significant implications for the recruitment and selection of staff in universities. Bearing in mind the financial implications of appointing new academic staff on anything other than short-term contracts (and acknowledging the negative side of these to both parties) the conservative approach to recruitment and selection taken by many heads gives cause for concern. While some may accept the idea of candidates giving a seminar or lecture, 'to suggest going beyond that is greeted with incredulity'. While appraiser training is now generally mandatory, training to chair or be a member of a selection committee rarely, if ever, is. Yet in workshop exercises conducted on ranking applicants for academic posts, heads' perceptions as to the suitability of different candidates differ markedly and when they discuss this in groups the achievement of consensus can be problematical. Moreover, when different groups compare outcomes, the proposed rankings are almost always different. This suggests that, as heads, we would be wise to consider a wider portfolio of selection techniques than those generally employed at present.

But many heads have little opportunity of recruiting new staff. Their main concern is to motivate existing staff. Believing that they have few carrots and no sticks, one of the greatest difficulties for heads (and a frequent role play in appraisal training) is the lecturer at the top of the scale who does just enough to avoid disciplinary procedures but is widely believed by colleagues to be 'swinging the lead'. The head is in a cleft stick for if s/he is seen to do nothing this reflects badly on departmental leadership. A survey of academics at different levels in several northern universities produced an interesting ranking of incentives in an exploration into what motivates academics. Many respondents showed frustration with their current situation, the following remarks being typical: 'the institution is collapsing' and, 'I need a greater sense that my research and teaching are valued'. In view of the fact that they have little flexibility in the allocation of financial rewards it may come as some comfort to hard-pressed heads of departments that additional increments did not rank first for any category of respondent. The only groups for whom financial incentives were particularly important were females who are likely to be lower on the pay scale, Grade A lecturers, and readers. Improvements in working conditions, particularly in regard to research opportunities, ranked first or second for nearly all categories. 'A PC on my desk' appeared to be an almost universally perceived motivator.

The comment from the lecturer who felt the need to be valued is a significant point. Although in appraisal training appraisers are urged to show appreciation of tasks accomplished and objectives met as well as affirmation of the individual, in practice this experience would appear to be quite rare. Or rather it is the perception of appraisees that their appraisers show little appreciation. Many find it both difficult to give and receive. Nevertheless, it is important, I believe, for heads to find ways of showing appreciation of colleagues. The growing evidence of stress-induced illness or near-illness in universities gives cause for concern. It occurs at all levels and raises both policy and resource issues for heads and more senior colleagues. An important aspect of my own learning in regard to the people side of departmental management has been a growing understanding of Jung's theory of psychological type as interpreted in the Myers Briggs Type Indicator. This has enabled me to have a greater understanding of colleagues with different personality types; of how they approach problems, how they seek to solve them, and what is likely to stress them. In the context of motivation I have become aware of how different temperaments prefer to be appreciated. The contrast between those who need regular, frequent appreciation from all levels of staff with whom they come into contact and who find it particularly difficult to receive negative criticism, and those who feel insulted by receiving appreciation for what they consider to be a routine task is considerable. While all people need to be appreciated, academics as a group probably find it as difficult as any either to give it or to receive it.

6. Appraisal and staff development

Academic staff appraisal has now been implemented in universities and in a number of institutions. The documentation has been modified at least once in order to implement changes found necessary or desirable after the system has been in practice for a year or more. Appraiser training was one of the earliest pieces of large-scale staff development undertaken in most universities. While the details of appraisal schemes vary from institution to institution, appraisal is, at least in the public domain, linked with staff development rather than with effective departmental management or staff assessment and promotion. However, even within a single institution the ethos can vary. A head of a large department may only appraise other appraisers, whereas in a smaller one s/he may appraise a number of staff. An incoming head of department may wish, over a two-year period, say, to appraise all members of academic staff in order to get to know them better. One new head commented that he had realized half-way through his second year that the staff appraised by him were better known to him than those who were not and made the suggestion, although it was not a requirement, that he should appraise all staff over a two-year cycle. An incoming head in another institution was warned against looking at the appraisal forms for colleagues 'as this was likely to reduce the level of trust which had developed between appraiser and appraisee'. This head had, therefore, to duplicate the system by personally interviewing each member of staff annually in order to learn more about their ideas, aspirations and anxieties. Whether appraisal is hierarchical or an extension of peer review, unless the head of department can meet with appraisers both before and after the interview cycle, as well as have access to the appraisal form, a major tool of human resource management in universities is lost.

An increasing number of departments build staff development events in to the academic year. My own department, for example, has a regular annual two-day 'retreat'. There is often a central theme to this event and the work, typically, consists partly of group work on an issue of concern to the department and partly of a presentation by an invited speaker on, for instance, academic peer review of teaching or equal opportunities. But for a department to achieve a behavioural change, let alone an attitudinal one, a greater investment of time and commitment will be required than this. In one department where a group of senior staff was keen to introduce peer review of teaching, this was only achieved following two full days of experiential learning for all academic staff, followed by some tough discussions at school committee. Quite rightly, academic staff wished to be assured of the complete separation of peer review from appraisal or promotion issues. With this understanding they agreed to the introduction of peer review of teaching for one year and for the system to be evaluated at the end of the year.

7. Communication

A number of heads of department believe lines of communication to and from the centre lack clarity. In some universities there is a belief that requests for information or for clarification are not responded to and heads are unclear about who is an appropriate point of contact for different issues. A number of heads feel that with the more managerial approach to university management there are inadequate opportunities for expressing points of view, that the senate has become a set piece and that the centre does not wish to hear from middle managers except through the formal decision-making machinery. There is often a strong suspicion that all matters of importance have been decided elsewhere. Some heads believe there to be inadequate opportunities for networking or perhaps it is that they have inadequate experience in this. Intra-organizational networking at head of department level is a valuable support mechanism for heads. This is something that women heads of department tend to do through external organizations perhaps, partly, because they are so outnumbered in any one single institution.

8. Time for research

All heads find it hard to allocate time for research. On being asked how much time they spent on research the responses of a group of heads from one institution ranged from 5 per cent to 60 per cent of their total available time. Most heads had developed a personal plan for research. Those in science and medicine claim that it is almost impossible to get back to leading-edge research after a period as a head of department, school, or dean. But most heads adopt a tactical plan for at least keeping in touch with research and some manage to be extremely productive. Tactics which heads have mentioned have included writing up the results of work undertaken before they were head of department, designing 'quick and dirty projects' which do not require long experiments or large data sets, being a team member in an externally-funded project with post-doctoral fellows undertaking the experimental work or fieldwork, or as more than one has put it, 'invading personal and family time' for research.

CONCLUSION

So how do heads of departments feel about being in this role? Is it one to be endured or enjoyed or both? Is it undertaken to relieve others of the management burden or is it undertaken because incumbents feel there is no other obvious candidate? Was there a strong sense of appointment by the centre? Qualitative evidence of views and feelings expressed and of the language used by heads of departments today suggests that, in the main, the role is 'owned'. There is a recognition that in the current educational environment a head of department needs to manage and nurture resources effectively for the common good – indeed for survival. More heads of departments are concerned to plan their careers; planning for after their term of office to move on to headship of school, deanship, or to become a pro-vice-chancellor; or aspire to return to effective and enjoyable teaching and research. Whatever plans a head has, s/he is currently preparing more effectively for that future by ensuring a continuous research focus, by seeking opportunities for wider management experience, by having a personal development plan, by becoming a reflective practitioner and allowing time for reflection.

It is, however, a lonely role. As one head reported, one's colleagues 'will have a go at you if you get it wrong but they will never tell you if you get it right'. The gratitude one head felt after an away day with a group of colleagues, one of whom stayed behind to give positive feedback, was all the greater for its rarity. A management team can give support; networking is valuable and those who engage in it, with confidentiality assured, learn from each other and provide consultation and group learning. It is less than ten years since the publication of the Jarratt Report (CVCP, 1985). In the years since 1985 universities have moved rapidly towards a recognition that 'the leadership of departments are key appointments'. In the complexity of managing a department or school in a university with fully delegated budgets, it is clear that 'the head of department must possess the requisite managerial capabilities'. Nevertheless, academic leadership is essential for departments aspiring to excellence in research and teaching. The head of department is both strategist and tactician. The working week has lengthened, many heads regularly working between 50 and 60 hours a week. This is not resented, it's just that, as one head said, 'there are many hours but some hours seem longer than others'.

NOTES

1. B Disraeli, speech in Edinburgh, 29 Oct 1867, cited in *Oxford Dictionary of Quotations*, Oxford.
2. Hereafter I will use the term 'head of department' to include 'head of school', or 'head' to include both.
3. To preserve the anonymity of respondent institutions and individuals, quotations and data will not be ascribed to specific universities and staff.
4. The Northern Universities Consortium.

REFERENCES

Beckhard, R and Harris, RT (1987) *Organisational Transitions*, Reading Mass: Addison-Wesley.

Bridges, W (1991) *Managing Transitions,* Reading Mass: Addison-Wesley.

Committee of Vice Chancellors and Principals (1985), *Report of the Steering Committee on Efficiency Studies in Universities* (Jarratt Report), London: CVCP.

Committee of Vice Chancellors and Principals (1989) *Academic Standards in Universities* (Reynolds Report), 3 vols., London: CVCP.

Mintzberg, H (1973), *The Nature of Managerial Work,* New York: Harper & Row.

Schön, D (1979) *The Reflective Practitioner,*New York: Basic Books.

PART THREE:

IMPLEMENTING CROSS-INSTITUTIONAL CHANGE

EDITORIAL COMMENT

An important feature of British further and higher education in recent years has been the growing tendency, resulting from a new emphasis on central mission statements and strategic planning, for policy initiatives which seek to promote change of different forms at a variety of levels across the entire institution. The contributions in Part Two have already pointed to the impact of such policies on departments. The following contributions move beyond the departmental level to consider a number of examples of leadership in cross-institutional policies and initiatives. Freda Tallantyre describes the approach which she adopted in directing an Enterprise in Higher Education project – an initiative which, as discussed in Chapter 1, was greeted with considerable suspicion in many quarters. She outlines the variety of strategies employed to overcome this hostility. In particular, she set out to highlight and build upon existing good practice in relevant areas, and to place a lot of emphasis on working with those who were enthusiastic or those likely to become convinced of the desirability of change, leaving the 'unwilling' to become more isolated – and also to be denied the additional resource which was an attractive feature of the Enterprise initiative. Not having managerial responsibility, the key roles for Freda Tallantyre and her team were to act as stimulus, broker and internal consultant. As other contributors also suggest, in some areas of change it is on occasion much easier to gain support from senior management and from the grass roots than it is from the middle tiers. The interconnected nature of change in higher education comes across strongly in this contribution as the Enterprise in Higher Education initiative was not intended to become a system of education in itself but a tool for confronting change constructively, its momentum being continued by, for example, linking in to credit accumulation and transfer schemes, open learning activities, developments in National Vocational Qualifications (NVQs), etc.

A second example of seeking to promote a cross-institutional approach without direct managerial authority is provided by Geoff Layer. As a result of his involvement in the development and delivery of a large credit accumulation and transfer scheme he became firmly committed to the importance of providing a comprehensive educational guidance and support service for students. This personal commitment coincided with changes taking place within the institution which created considerably more choice for the student body. In a situation with devolved budgeting, one of the key challenges he faced was convincing academic departments that a new central support service was essential to cater for the diversity of students and their programmes. From a fixed pool of money this meant that resources would have to come from somewhere else in the university, requiring a large scale 'persuasion' exercise. The main argument used related to the potential benefits to the student body. However, if the 'carrot' of bettering the lot of students did not work there was always the 'big stick' of funding! Because funding of higher and further education seems set to become more closely linked to successful student completion (as opposed to initial enrolment), guidance to ensure that students are admitted to the programmes that best suit their needs, and are given all the support necessary once they are on a programme to complete it successfully, rapidly achieves a high priority for the institution, with implications of change across the whole system.

Ian Todd, in contrast, as vice-principal of a large college of further education, is in a direct management role; persuasion, however, is also his key to implementing change. The task which he and his colleagues shared was that of providing a quality educational experience for students in the light of a declining unit of resource. The challenge he addresses is how to develop a strategy which reduces staff costs, increases the size of classes, yet does not diminish the quality of the educational experience – a tall order! He graphically illustrates the importance in times of change of moving beyond traditional reactions and ways of thinking. Thus, increasing class size, for example, may not automatically have a detrimental effect if it releases resources which can be used to support better tutorial or independent study facilities. This chapter illustrates how the emphasis on the 'bottom line' forces managers in colleges and universities to increasingly apply ingenuity and creativity as they seek to protect the quality of the student experience.

The key question is whether there is a level below which all the creativity in the world will not be sufficient to overcome the problems created by lack of investment.

Chapter 7

Using Projects for Dynamic Intervention in the Curriculum of Higher Education

Freda Tallantyre

CLIMATE AND CONTEXT

Project funding has become, in recent years, a major incentive used by the government to register its priorities for the agenda of education and training organizations, more frequently channelled through the Employment Department than the Department for Education because of the increasing preoccupation with vocational education. Such funding has proved increasingly attractive to bidding organizations in the face of an otherwise dwindling unit of resource. It has an advantage, for the government, of encouraging ownership by contractors, by comparison with externally imposed but unfunded initiatives; the response to the school-based Technical and Vocational Education Initiative or to Enterprise in Higher Education, compared to the response to Standard Assessment Tasks for schools, reminds us that the carrot is usually more effective than the stick. Moreover, although it may seem regrettable, most change in education has been generated from external rather than internal sources, because of a natural conservatism that developed while the sector was far less publicly accountable than is currently the case.

The problems of project funding for educational institutions include the fact that the resource and time-scale are often insufficient to do more than introduce superficial change, and that it can deflect them from or even conflict with their true priorities. The University of Northumbria at Newcastle (UNN) cannot claim never to have pursued external funding simply because it was there. However, in the case of Enterprise in Higher Education, the time was right, the theme fit the university mission, the money was a substantial £1 million and the time scale of five years would allow for some real development and learning within the organization. A proposal for funding, in response to an invitation to bid from the Employment Department in 1988, was submitted prior to my involvement. In practice, the impact of the EHE initiative proved even more influential in terms of management of institutional change than had been originally anticipated. This project is used for the remainder of this chapter as a case to demonstrate external intervention in the higher education curriculum.

The Enterprise concept that graduates of higher education should be flexible and effective in terms of transferable personal skills for their future contexts, and in particular work, was destined to be highly acceptable to most of the former polytechnics, with their largely vocational and applied curriculum. The vice-chancellor of UNN had already written of the importance of competence, alongside knowledge, for graduates and was one of a small group who encouraged the Secretary of State for Education at the time to initiate EHE. There existed within the university a solid foundation of experience of working alongside employers, as clients for continuing professional development, and as partners in offering work placements within degree and diploma courses. Simultaneously, the first year of EHE was to be the first year of incorporation, and the former Newcastle Polytechnic was gearing up to become more business-like in managing its own operations and finances. The mission, which had been written for the newly independent polytechnic, committed itself to 'the development of the full human potential of its students and to their better preparation for employment, through the development not only of intellectual abilities but also enterprise, competencies and personal skills...'.[1] Consequently, the proposal for funding was developed with complete support from the top, and talked of 'accelerating change' rather than introducing it.

DEVELOPING THE PROPOSAL

The levels of autonomy and devolution which have prevailed in many universities often make them rather slow in decision-making. An externally-driven schedule for submission of bids was, on this occasion then, helpful in focusing the minds of an institutionally representative task group, chaired by a dean. It conducted an adequate amount of consultation with staff and employers to arrive at a definition of enterprise education which would be acceptable, around which the project framework was then swiftly designed and submitted. It is probably fair to admit, in retrospect, that the third major group of stakeholders, ie, the students themselves, were imperfectly consulted at the time, and it is one measure of how far our own understandings of enterprise deepened that student-led initiatives became amongst the most dynamic in the later stages of the project.

By October 1988 UNN was selected to participate, with ten other universities and polytechnics, from 82 proposing institutions, and was the second to sign a contract. Being in the first round offered advantages in terms of high national profile, and strong identity with other participating institutions, but also imposed burdens of working without precedents, under heavy external evaluation, and of being rapidly required to induct and support a second round of participants.

DIRECTING THE PROJECT

It is necessary to speak personally for a time, since being a 'change agent' is not a role embraced by all, and it may be helpful to identify some of the indicative qualities. I recall vividly the initial shock when my then head of department suggested to me that I might consider applying for the job of directing EHE. It would be nice to claim that, like a real entrepreneur, I had an immediate vision of its potential, but that was not the truth. I had been very peripheral in the development of the proposal, and had certainly anticipated through my own response the resistance that academics would demonstrate to an initiative called 'enterprise'. Many interpreted it initially as a plot to subvert the values and critical objectivity of higher education into a narrow, conformist business mentality. In the event, there followed for me an immensely valuable week of absorption in the proposal to unpick the implications of the term 'enterprise' and realize its true possibilities, because it prepared me to lead others empathetically from misplaced repugnance to dawning opportunity.

What was it that might equip me for such a job? My background was in adult education and access to higher education, which at first sight seemed like a different agenda. I had come on secondment to Newcastle Polytechnic in order to facilitate flexible part-time study for mature students through the first credit accumulation and transfer scheme, outside the Council for National Academic Awards. That had given me good experience of initiating without predecessors, and of project management. However, after two years of opening access, I had increased my consciousness that getting adults into higher education was only the first hurdle; offering them an appropriate curriculum, learning and assessment styles, and taking their experience into account were aspects beyond mere structures for study. Within EHE I found a coincident concern for flexibility and saw opportunities for empowerment of students, to help them move from dependency to independency.

Through my ten years of previous experience working with largely unemployed people, I had been obliged to address feedback that urged needs, confirming Maslow's hierarchy, to improve one's economic and social situation and self-respect by finding work, before being able to relax with the personal development offered by education. Enterprise offered to equip people with the skills that would make them effective in obtaining and performing a job, and also in taking better control over their own lives.

My work with a voluntary adult education organization, with flat career structures and tight resources, had skilled me in networking with other organizations to achieve more by pooling resources, in identifying who the key people were to influence things, and in getting to them. I had learned to listen carefully to find the 'fit' in our agenda and to negotiate collaboration. Counselling training and experience helped me understand people, their motivations, and that there are many roads to the same destination. Outreach education in far-flung rural and impoverished industrial environments had posed a rich array of problems to be solved.

With a jolt, I realized that the skills and resources I had had to draw upon, and those which my former students most required, were the very same that were being described as 'enterprising'. Two years of secondment to the polytechnic had given me the opportunity to test those skills in a very different but equally challenging culture, but had not wiped out the freshness of perspective I brought from one sector to another. This combination often proved effective in situations of change.

Most of my working life had been spent trying to help students face difficult challenges and change things for themselves. When the vice-chancellor threw down the gauntlet in interview and said, 'If you like an easy life, this job is not for you', I knew this challenge was mine and I had to do it.

ANALYSING THE CULTURE

The first step was to sit back and take stock of what I had learned about the culture of the institution in my two years. Newcastle Polytechnic was one of the largest in the sector, with a reputation for quality that can make for complacence; it would require assurance that the baby would not be thrown out with the bath water.

However, it was still reeling from changes in internal structure, with the identity of new teams still ill-formed; here was an opportunity to contribute resource to engender a positive spirit through early collaborative achievement, if one could avoid it being perceived as just one more burden. But still more change was on the horizon, with incorporation moving the institution from a bureaucratic local authority management to a more managerial internal climate. The burden of responsibility would require a more assertive executive, and change agents would need to avoid contributing to a sense of prescription and imposition from the top by being seen to offer solutions to problems and ways for staff at the coal-face to deal constructively with new terms and conditions and diminishing resources.

The development of a corporate identify and strong leadership would be difficult in an organization welded together only 20 years previously from separate colleges, from which many senior staff still occupied positions of responsibility within the polytechnic. The climate had long been one of devolved authority, with a soft touch from the centre, and now there was to be devolution to faculty cost centres and inclusion of the deans with the directorate in a formal executive. The existing tension between the centre and the faculty baronies was destined to increase, especially where resources were concerned. As a consequence, a centrally directed project could expect backing, rather than leadership, from the top, and would need to be thinly resourced at the centre to be perceived by faculties and departments as a resource opportunity rather than a threat.

One must not assume, however, that the baronies themselves, nor even the manorial settlements within them, were homogeneous. Each had its own culture and language to learn, often deriving more from its associated profession (eg, the law, the health service, the Engineering Council) than from an educational establishment. A broad knowledge of them was deeply enriched by spending a large part of the first six months in-post in carrying out an informal but detailed audit of current enterprise practice around the institution through reading course documentation and conducting intensive interviews with around 50 course leaders. The purpose of these discussions was mainly to listen respectfully to the objectives of the course teams, identify areas ripe for development and raise awareness of enterprise by relating its potential specifically to aspirations already on the agenda in order to turn them into priorities. The dialogue had to be rooted in their terminology and values; different overhead transparencies were prepared for more formal awareness-raising sessions delivered, for example, to engineers on one occasion, and to sociologists on another.

Fortunately, the concept of enterprise was itself highly flexible and a variety of shades of interpretation could be admitted from around the institution in defining the indefinable without too far distorting its essential spirit (Tavistock Institute, 1989). It was clear from the start that in such a climate, enterprise developments would be kaleidoscopic – rich, colourful and, if well managed, with distinctive patterns, rather than fragmented.

It is important to bear in mind that being 'professional' in a polytechnic culture is more often associated with the profession into which one's students graduate, rather than with the teaching profession. This factor had the advantage of offering many ready-made external partners amongst employers, but the disadvantage that pedagogical development was not of primary interest to staff, especially since academic recruitment, promotion and distinction have been more regularly associated with a research rather than a teaching profile. Enterprise in Higher Education was to be very much an educational development project. However, teaching had been the central pole of the mission statement and the basis for the institutional reputation for quality.

One helpful development had been the recent revamping of a service, previously concerned more with technical aids to teaching, into one of the best resourced educational development services in the sector, concerned with curricular and pedagogical innovation. These staff provided an important set of allies, working in tandem with EHE on staff development and evaluation throughout the project. Another set was discovered in a group of faculty-based staff servicing many courses for communication skills. Their operation was to be dignified by recognition as a separate communication unit and reinforced by additional staff, partly as a result of EHE, which meant they were well disposed to assist. Allies are a vital linchpin in change-making initiatives, especially when central resourcing is to be slim and much must be achieved by negotiation with other agencies.

DEVISING A STRATEGY

It appeared important that if 'enterprise', which was essentially a dynamic and experiential style of education, was significantly to infuse courses, then staff would need first to experience it for themselves; the theory should inform the developmental practices and procedures of the project. At the same time, the proposal had made clear that integration of EHE was the intention, so it would be folly to overlook existing systems and procedures where they accommodated the initiative.

In the event, few existing systems were appropriate initially, though some were beneficial at later stages for embedding, eg, validation and review, about which more is said below. Interestingly, the new systems which EHE invented proved often so much more motivational that, by the end of the project, several have been adopted at an institutional level for managing future change.

One mechanism which was well understood was cross-institutional committees, and one such structure had been built into the project proposal for its coordination, at a sub-steering level. It seemed that this would be useful for generating ownership, raising awareness and identifying networks of interested activists. However, it also seemed necessary to avoid the greatest risk of committee structures – that they can become debating societies – so the enterprise coordinating group was to be given a key task of approving development proposals. This exercise was readily understood, from the experience of validation panels, but it was moulded to be swifter and more formative a meeting between proposers and approvers.

It was also possible to pick up the familiar tool of the working party for development of particular arms of the strategy, such as staff development, evaluation, materials and resources and publicity. However, these were kept much smaller than usual – a few key activists were given a remit to act rather than report – and were rapidly wound up when their action was no longer necessary. This was where the most dependable inner network of EHE was cultivated.

To give credit and recognition for existing good practice and quality relevant to EHE, it appeared useful to offer internal rather than external role models at the beginning. This would allow for cumulative development, and diffuse the challenge from some corners that 'we do that already'. A proactive staff development programme of weekly half-day workshops was built around 'state of the art' practice, and evolved with the project itself. It seemed counterproductive to prescribe attendance, so staff (and employer partners) came out of interest but, controversially, their departments were paid to release them. Though this seemed to break the normal convention of paying, rather than being paid, for staff development, it overcame the real hurdle of obtaining for it sufficient priority and real time amid an increasingly pressured workload. The programme brought together activists from across institutional boundaries, creating alternative networks of support which were more formally capitalized upon from year two by facilitating networks which set their own agenda and action around themes like placements, portfolios and numeracy.

While these programmes nurtured and supported individual activists, it was also essential to acknowledge that ideas must be tied into action, and action could only be achieved with team assent. Collaborative activity was, therefore, stimulated by promoting the 'away-day' opportunity, for course or departmental teams to pick up relevant ideas and go off-site for a day or more, often with employer partners, to work out what these might mean in curricular or pedagogical terms. These team days proved so directly and interpersonally productive that they have become a key stratagem in the management by departments of their own staff development.

When aspirations were sufficiently well developed, course teams would bring to the enterprise coordinating group a proposal for their own learning contract. The advantages were that learning objectives had been identified for and owned by themselves, and would subsequently be managed independently, with the same skills that we were expecting students to develop. However, the 'contract' was also a business-like concept that required them to justify, plan, evaluate and be accountable for their progress. After a few initial worries about such an unfamiliar mechanism, such as whether signing the contract would mean personal liability for resources if the plan were not delivered to time or to the letter, this approach became the linchpin of the entire project. It absorbed the majority of resources, encouraged an entrepreneurial style amongst staff, and was subsequently adopted by the university as a basis for stimulating other kinds of change against a development fund.

To make this approach work had meant taking a calculated risk of circumventing resource managers, like deans and heads of department, to direct resource and power for action straight to the people responsible for course design and teaching. The course leader, not even identified in the management tree at the time, was in fact the key target. The effect was powerful, since staff at this level often felt disempowered and undervalued. However, it was probably less contested then than it might have been subsequently because heads of department were still struggling themselves to accept the 'management' garb, especially in terms of resources. Later in the project, it became useful to let heads know what funding remained ring-fenced for their potential use, and to use their leadership to stimulate further bids.

Although targets for development had been identified within the proposal in accordance with the cycle by which courses came up for validation or review, it was quickly found to be more realistic to work along the spectrum from 'enthusiastic' to 'emergent' and through to 'unwilling' modernizers, as identified by the Tavistock Institute (1989). The enthusiastic were able to fully engage with developments and produce good models for transfer; the emergent could become convinced of the feasibility and work at a more cautious pace; and the unwilling would ultimately feel more isolated and denied resource. As long as quantitative targets were met for each year, the sponsor was happy, and eventually no department remained aloof from the initiative.

The key roles played by my allies and myself, since we could only influence and negotiate, proved to be stimulus, broker and internal consultant. To be a stimulus meant listening for and highlighting opportunity; to be a broker meant offering guidance in developing a suitable proposal and acting as an advocate for it when it was submitted to the enterprise coordinating group; to be an internal consultant meant spending time observing practice and collecting feedback from participants, which was then offered to course teams for them to prioritize needs, and workshop days were designed to help them develop ways to address them. These central players derived their own support from one another and the invaluable national network of EHE staff which developed over the lifetime of the project as a whole.

One aspect of the strategy in which we improved as time went on, but were never wholly successful, was in devising really simple administrative procedures which would have made engagement with the project more comprehensible and accessible. There was an obligation to use rather bureaucratic internal financial procedures and regular information collection for external accountability. Furthermore, we invented rather complex formulae for calculating resource potentially available to teams which would protect our ability to support all comers, in line with contract targets. Grass roots teaching staff had little experience of handling existing administrative systems and were puzzled by new ones, so that they sometimes penalized themselves by failing to claim for resource to which they were entitled. It should have been possible to set up a more enterprising system.

SUSTAINING MOMENTUM

Development proposals were not comprehensive in terms of enterprise, but focused on aspects which were of primary importance to proposers. However, success in one area usually prompted evolutionary development into others, and the challenge became to offer sufficient support for continuing enthusiasts while simultaneously bringing in new participants.

An invaluable aid became the Materials and Resources Centre for Enterprising Teaching (MARCET), a flexible open learning centre for staff which allowed them to work, individually or in teams, on curricular development at their own pace and with their own focus. The university has opted to continue funding the facility after the project, and to extend its focus to embrace all aspects of educational development, apart from subject-specific content.

Although staff undertaking developments were given the resource to provide real time for their work, other rewards and incentives were rarely material. There were those who submitted their innovations for small internal awards, through Alternative Learning Week, or external, through the Partnership Awards, for example, but even then it was recognition that was the greatest motivator. Successful projects were given a high profile, through the staff development programme, network activity, the project newsletter, internal publications called 'Red guides', and conference presentations. Staff enjoyed the unusual value attached to their teaching expertise and began to add their achievements to cvs. After five years, there is empirical evidence to suggest that these are recognized further in appraisal, and have contributed to some promotions. The disappearance of the binary line did, however, revive a competing status for research activity, but at least educational development itself has made a mark on the research agenda.

As the less willing modernizers saw the benefits reaped by other participants, heard the positive feedback from students or read the favourable HMI reports on EHE practice, they became more receptive.

The programme itself had to evolve each year, both to offer new opportunities and to engage with new understandings and external pressures. The proactive staff development programme and learning contracts of year 1 were supplemented by away-days, MARCET and Alternative Learning Week in year 2. Networks followed in year 3, opportunities for central departments in year 4, and a final gold rush in year 5. An early concern with development of transferable personal skills led to an emerging interest in accrediting experiential learning, and from there to articulating its outcomes, and thence to compatibility with National Vocational Qualifications. A key focus in one year was assessment, in another, Europe. By such means interest was kept alive after the initial novelty had worn off. Moreover, although much of the general direction could be anticipated, it was often found that incremental steps were more realistic in allowing staff to pace change.

USING MANAGEMENT

Although most progress was achieved by persuasion and negotiation, it was important to know when and how to use management structures. While I revelled in the autonomy afforded me, I learned the value of regular monthly meetings with my line manager, the deputy chief executive, to identify institutional changes that needed making and to obtain a direct voice into the executive. It also proved useful to keep him involved as a member of the enterprise policy group, and latterly as its chair, so that he could hear directly and respond to the views of powerful external partners. I also had valuable termly meetings with the vice-chancellor himself, to update him on progress generally or to focus on key themes and issues.

The enterprise policy group itself steered the programme with a grouping of mainly employer partners. They were frequently puzzled by the culture and operation of higher education, and much patient effort had to be mutually expended to reach common understandings. The group proved, however, an invaluable resource, to attract interest and participation from external communities, to offer fresh perspectives and the experience of alternative cultures, and as a lever from the marketplace to move internal obstacles. It was beneficial to make them directly accountable to the institutional board of governors, who themselves comprised senior representatives of regional organizations. Employer representation on the coordinating group and on occasional working parties proved equally valuable in posing critical questions for and offering alternative suggestions to innovators.

As the internal management team became more consolidated post-incorporation, it became more possible and effective to deliver management development. Faculty and departmental boards were frequently used as a forum to discuss issues and potential, and special management seminars were arranged on subjects such as total quality management, and NVQs.

The fact that enterprise was established as an institutional policy from the start was an immensely helpful lever, but to have it properly understood and monitored it became important to achieve representation in key committees, such as quality improvement and academic standards, and course proposals. Moreover, it became necessary for integration and embedding purposes to develop complementary policies, eg, a regional policy, and a corporate staff development and training strategy.

EVALUATING ACHIEVEMENT

In the context of integration, it was essential to use the existing arrangements for course validation and review in order to have attention paid systematically to development across the whole institution. The danger inherent in this approach is that it sometimes calls forth a somewhat rhetorical and superficial response to change, but this is a small price to pay for the broad ownership created by holding panel chairs responsible, rather than the project team, and for the resulting cross-fertilization.

External evaluation by the sponsor remained at a demanding, but rather unsatisfactory, level throughout the project, focusing more on process and quantitative indicators than on qualitative development and outcomes. This often created bureaucratic pressures upon innovators to produce data which they found lacking in meaning, and threatened at times to deter participation.

Internal evaluation sought to focus more upon qualitative findings, and to create dynamic feedback loops, through staff development and publications, to stimulate continuous improvement. The culmination of this was an additional evaluation project which was able to offer sustained development assistance to six course teams, and to extrapolate lessons for the whole learning community. The experience has been able to influence evaluation practice in the university as a whole, though it was too resource-intensive to retain in its entirety.

A large-scale monitoring exercise, conducted as part of the internal project evaluation, reflected in the final report interesting and significant findings about the impact of the project over the five years in terms of opportunities for students to develop 'enterprising' skills, and to experience innovative learning and assessment approaches.[2] It will be able to influence future practice in the university, though it is perhaps regrettable that we did not establish it in such a way as to have a more dramatic effect within the life of our own EHE programme. Nationally, however, it is probably one of the most sustained studies, involving large numbers of students.

Conflicting and complementary agenda

One of the most enduring values of EHE is that it has not become a system of education in itself, but rather a tool for confronting change constructively and remaining dynamic. As a consequence, it has been vital to work with concurrent pressures, to find ways of coping with them and to find further opportunities in complementary agenda.

When our EHE proposal was devised, modern language skills were not included within our objectives, but with 1992 within our project schedule, European skills and curricula became priority components.

The government targets to increase participation in higher education threatened to invalidate the experiential methods we had developed that were most effective for small groups. However, we launched a network and a newsletter to promote creative ways to get participation in large groups, urged peer assessment as a way of sharing the burden and introduced peer support groups through supplemental instruction.

Our university's decision to unitize the curriculum now challenges us to preserve the coherent development of skills within discrete modules, and to build new kinds of team identities for staff and students.

We have constantly sought additional resource and opportunities to develop more extensively complementary initiatives, such as projects on Learning Outcomes and Credits, Accreditation of Work-Based Learning (Employment Department), Accreditation of Open Learning in Companies (Training and Enterprise Councils) and Educational Technology (Higher Education Funding Council for England). Some developments, such as NVQs, both complement and conflict with EHE, and we have endeavoured, by being proactive, to influence the shape of them before they impact directly at our levels.

To tackle the potential conflict between teaching and research, exacerbated by the removal of the binary line, we have attempted to raise the status of pedagogical research in its own right, with the additional benefit of enhancing professional pride.

Effecting change from the middle of organizations

Some of the key lessons to emerge from this experience for middle managers appear to me, then, to be the following.

From the middle one cannot directly change the culture, but rather seek to influence it. An early imperative, therefore, is to get to know the existing culture (or more likely cultures, in higher education) and to identify the key resources, functions, activists and motivators that can make things happen.

If you are fortunate, the innovation for which you are responsible will run with, rather than against, the grain in the organization's strategy; but where this is not obviously the case, it is helpful to find minor 'matches', in which your agenda can support the achievement of other objectives. Success is more likely to follow where you are perceived as empowering others to act, and by getting to those who have the skills to act, they may frequently bring along for you their managers who have the power to act.

Having some small resource to back innovations is helpful beyond all proportion to its size. It is viewed as a bonus to be won, and an investment in staff creativity, which consequently brings an even greater return in terms of time and energy. It also ensures priority over unresourced initiatives.

Once you have enabled people to make progress, it becomes important to recognize and reward that innovation, often achievable by not very expensive means. However, in this respect higher education seems to have more to learn, especially for rewarding excellence in teaching.

Finally, it became clearer to me later in the programme that innovators very rarely have a crystal-clear vision of where they want to get to. 'Vision', indeed, often proves to be a synthesis of what has been seen and heard elsewhere. However, innovators do appear to develop strong intuitions, and those who are successful have learned to trust these and to take the concomitant risks of where they will lead them.

To return briefly, and in conclusion, to the personal, as director of EHE I realized quickly that I was being offered one of the most important opportunities, as well as challenges, of my life. It is difficult, especially for women, to break through the glass ceiling into senior management of higher education. Such a programme, which places one at the frontiers of change and development and yet requires one to achieve through influence rather than direct authority, develops both the skills and confidence to manage at the highest levels. It stimulates vision, requires an holistic understanding and allows access to senior personnel, internal and external, for direct or indirect mentoring.

The main danger to be avoided is becoming identified as 'the change agent' and so having all new agendas laid at one's door, with the possible consequences of losing the integrity with others of being identified with particular principles and values, and of burn-out for oneself. The way forward for me has been to step into a more conventional management role, which nevertheless allows opportunities to direct initiatives which evolve naturally from EHE, while managing a larger team who themselves need the same scope and encouragement to innovate as was afforded to me.

NOTES

1. *The Mission*, Newcastle Polytechnic, 1987.
2. *Enterprise in Higher Education: Final Report*, University of Northumbria at Newcastle, 1993.

REFERENCE

Tavistock Institute (1989) *Organisation and Management of EHE: Working Paper No.2, Case Study Evaluation of the EHE Initiative,* London: Tavistock Institute of Human Relations.

Chapter 8

Student Guidance and Support – Changing the Approach

Geoff Layer

INTRODUCTION

It's the students who are important and they are the reason we took this job.

We will have heard this statement and variants of it on many occasions. In addition to their research duties, most staff in universities and colleges see themselves as being there to help the student. Much of this belief is based on a desire to help and also our own memories of the support we received. How many times have we heard people talking of schoolday memories and remember the support given by a particular teacher? We sometimes forget the breakdowns in the system but remember the good parts. Many of us see ourselves as carrying forward the work of that particular role model. Conversely, of course, the motivation behind wanting to help students may be because of the absence of any real support that staff had experienced themselves as students.

Times are changing for students and we need to recognize that change, plan for now and develop a strategy for the future. The changes needed are forced upon the system through funding and curriculum developments, alongside changing student perceptions.

This chapter addresses the existing framework for support and guidance in further and higher education, and identifies the reasons why major changes are needed. It provides an account of how one institution came, in a time of resource constraints, to make a significant new investment in the establishment of a division of access and guidance. The chapter is based upon my own experiences within a particular university and from discussions, presentations and analysis with colleagues in other institutions. On a personal level, this experience has seen a move from the role of a traditional academic teaching my subject (law), supporting students, researching and publishing through to a series of challenging new roles. I believe the starting point of being an academic within a department seeking to change the institutional approach was of fundamental importance. This gave me credibility with my colleagues by being seen to propose particular changes, not as a result of external pressures or directives from senior management, but because they were sound educationally and 'good ideas' in themselves.

The university developed from a traditional course-based institution that over a short period of time sought to widen participation through a concerted access strategy and increased curriculum flexibility. I was responsible for the implementation of the access strategy through working with local colleges to create specific progression routes for adult returners and groups under-represented in higher education. This was one of my first insights into the inadequacy of the guidance framework within higher education. While students received good support from local colleges, the actual transition into higher education posed them with a genuine culture shock. This meant that we had to review the provision for this group of students and ensure their guidance and support needs were addressed. It was, however, specific provision on the margins and never considered in the light of the whole institution.

The major factor in influencing a change in this situation came with the development of a flexible curriculum through a credit-based framework. The university was one of the pioneers of a credit-based curriculum. It introduced a common unit of curriculum currency and enabled students to negotiate courses that fitted their own objectives by varying the course pattern of the institution. I was responsible for the introduction and consequent management of this credit framework. A scheme such as this challenges the whole notion of student support and guidance and the university rapidly moved to a clear understanding that, having created a student choice framework, it needed to make sure that the choice was an informed one. The need to address the whole student guidance and support framework was the real challenge.

I believe that three factors were crucial in facilitating my own position in assisting the implementation of this change. The first was a strong sense of commitment from senior management to ensure that the policy was debated, agreed and supported. The second was that in my various roles I have always been an active member of the institutional committee structure and was able to ensure that pertinent issues were considered and agreed at different levels. The third, and probably the most important, was that I kept up a teaching commitment within my own discipline and was seen by colleagues to be going through the same process of change as them. This is vital to the concept of 'taking people with you' and lessens the danger of having a 'phantom' system where there is sound policy agreement on change but no delivery because staff have simply 'filed it' and hoped it would go away.

THE CONTEXT

Higher education has seen a number of rapid and wide-ranging changes in the last few years. It is interesting to note how some of these changes have affected institutions. There has been the incorporation of polytechnics which meant that they became separate legal entities and were no longer maintained through local councils. There has been a dramatic increase in the number of students staying in education after the age of 16, and higher education in particular has grown rapidly. Institutions have concentrated on mission statements, the creation of marketing departments and adopting a more managerial approach. It is only three years ago that I listened to a vice-chancellor talking about the strategic plan for his university. He talked for 45 minutes indicating how things were going to change, how they were going to be national and international market leaders, etc. During the entire talk *students* were not referred to once. The pace of change means that such an approach has rapidly become dated and unacceptable.

The support needs of students are rapidly coming to the top of institutional agendas and there is a realization that the systems that have 'served' students for years require a radical overhaul. However, as we are working in a period of resource restraint the only way to resource learner support effectively is to take resource from other areas. Needless to say the budget-holders are very concerned to ensure that it does not come from their budgets. This becomes the major challenge. How can we divert funding from one part of the institution to another? It is relatively easy to argue such financial changes on the basis of student numbers and new courses but an untried and additional service that affects everyone raises more difficulties. All the heads of department will immediately take the view that they can 'do' all the learner support and do not need any central interference and certainly are not going to pay for a central service. They will, of course, also say that they need more money to do it.

This is representative of another change that has taken place in many institutions, that of devolved budgets and cost centres. While there are many good reasons to devolve financial responsibility to those providing the local service it does create a tension between 'local' and institutional priorities. While this can be addressed to some extent through corporate planning and objective-setting it can be difficult to implement on the ground. This is even more the case if the budget-holders are resistant to the change, or unclear about a development.

So we had to take the budget-holders with us. We had to convince them of the need for change and demonstrate the positive outcomes. This required leadership from the top of the institution and successful ground work at the grass roots level. The grass roots support can be the easiest to achieve and if worked at long enough and hard enough the change is accepted before it is formally agreed.

To win the grass roots support we had to present the proposed change as being one of benefit to the students and one that enhances the quality of the student experience. Once the change becomes accepted at this level the battle is essentially won because most of the change is one of culture, so when it has been accepted by staff on the ground the culture automatically begins to change.

WHY IS GUIDANCE AND SUPPORT IMPORTANT?

For every student who withdraws from a course there is an argument that the education system has failed that individual. But have we? The individual may have been advised not to follow that particular course as it was felt that they were not ready for it. The individual may have rejected that advice because that was the only course they wanted to follow or it was the one their friends wanted to do. Students find it far easier to take advice on the way they write essays, present information, argue and other 'academic' matters than they do to take more general advice. This may be because the latter will tend to give options and choices whereas the former is more of a definitive statement from the individual tutor and much more difficult to challenge. It may also be due to the general perception that guidance is seen as a 'soft service' that has never been fully thought through on an institutional basis.

So what are the factors that we shared with colleagues to begin the process of change? In my experience there are six topics or issues which have been important in seeking to persuade colleagues of the necessity of introducing a comprehensive guidance and support system for students in higher education: funding, quality assurance, curriculum flexibility, class size, student charters, and student services. I shall discuss each in turn.

Funding

Following an Audit Commission/Office for Standards in Education report (Audit Office/OFSTED, 1993) on post-16 education, which demonstrated low completion rates, the Further Education Funding Council (FEFC) altered the traditional funding model. Colleges for years have been rewarded for recruiting more students. This has been measured in terms of the number of enrolments completed by the Further Education Statistical Return (FESR) date in early November. The performance indicator was merely the number of students recruited, not whether they actually succeeded on that course.

In order to boost recruitment colleges would offer as broad a programme of courses as possible, knowing that many courses would not recruit enough students to run but wanting to provide the opportunity for take-up. This strategy led to many new courses running for the first time and encouraged many to return to education or to stay on after 16. The strategy did not enable colleges to confidently predict enrolment and to manage student numbers alongside resources. Although the recruitment will have been undertaken with integrity there has always been the pressure to ensure that the course runs and that enrolment is buoyant.

Students who did not complete courses represented both a loss of opportunity, as in many cases the student was on an inappropriate course, and a loss of public funds as resources had been allocated to teach students who were leaving the course. The FEFC therefore introduced a funding model which included an element of 'outcome-related' funding. In essence the college would no longer be funded on the basis of the student enrolment but on an additional criteria of how many students were actually achieving their objectives and the amount of guidance they required.

Once such a model was identified and the concept of guidance appeared to be gaining national recognition, there was understandable delight from those involved in educational guidance circles as they presumed they would receive more resources. However, the FEFC was not allocating additional funds; the size of the cake was still the same and expansion was demanded. The FEFC was in effect saying that students must be supported better because if they leave, the college's funding would be affected. This outcome-related funding model effectively challenges colleges to develop a more coherent guidance and support framework.

It was not long before the Higher Education Funding Councils also took up the question of output-related funding. For many years higher education was funded on student enrolments within a strategic plan with enrolment rather than completion being the crucial statistic. It is not difficult to predict a future where universities, like colleges of further education, will also be funded on the basis of the number of students completing courses/credits as opposed to the number enrolling. The issues involved in this approach have recently been explored in a national development project commissioned by the Higher Education Quality Council (Robertson, 1994). If such a strategy does emerge then it is crucial to the financial viability of the university that as many students complete as possible. This does not mean that standards should be adjusted – they must be stringently observed – but that the guidance and support framework should be explicitly developed.

To my mind therefore, the future was clear. There was to be no more money and we must serve our students better. This was a key argument which I employed in seeking to make the case for investment in a comprehensive new access and guidance and support service. Staff are very aware of the funding strategies and they realize that there is no pot of gold coming. We all knew that the Funding Councils were shaping the type of educational provision through the funding model. We used this to persuade staff that the level of resource will be greater if we keep our students than it would be if they left. The loss of revenue in some universities through students withdrawing in the first year can be in excess of £1 million. This is income that can be spent on student support and lead to a major improvement in the student experience. The question staff tend to relate to is not whether we can afford to move in this way but more importantly, can we afford not to.

Quality assurance

Retention rates have long been a major part of the quality assurance processes of colleges and universities. It is central to the notion of a quality service that the students' expectations and needs are met. The traditional means of receiving student feedback are through questionnaires and staff/student meetings. Results of such processes are then evaluated and changes introduced as appropriate. Some of these processes though are questionable in respect of what can really be gleaned from the student perception. For example, at Sheffield Hallam University a student experience survey was undertaken of all first year students (Sheffield Hallam University, 1989). Seventy per cent stated that they would recommend the university to their friends. While this appears to be a very positive statement it has to be viewed alongside the fact that the students had experienced little of the university by the date of the survey (two terms) and the vast majority had never been to another university to enable a comparison.

The quality assurance system is an important part of the 'converting of minds' process. Staff know that quality assurance systems are open and public and they have a sense of pride in wanting to be seen to do a good job. Staff are generally committed to providing a good learning experience for students and appreciate that in order to achieve recognition for work it needs to be explicitly referred to in the quality assurance system. Consequently, the more the system refers specifically to learner support the more it is addressed by course teams and therefore there becomes greater acceptance of issues such as guidance.

Many staff/student meetings see an element of closing of ranks by staff who are working under great pressure and realize some of their collective shortcomings in respect of the student experience. Although some of the students are very vocal and pursue issues, a large majority tend to be quiet and conscious of the distinction between student and assessor. Many of the students have received little briefing or training for this role and are unaware not only of what is expected of them but of their rights in the management of the course.

It is interesting to note that student feedback and the mechanisms an institution has for receiving and acting upon it are now part of the FEFC college inspection system and are increasingly forming part of Higher Education Quality Council's quality audit process.

Curriculum flexibility

As the curriculum generally becomes more flexible and students study the same module/unit as part of different courses then the traditional models of guidance and support are challenged. If a student is to be given curriculum choice then that choice needs to be an informed choice. The student needs to know what is available, what they can do and the consequences of their choice. The student needs to operate in a framework where the language of choice and the awareness of that choice is commonly understood.

Students have traditionally been supported by course teams who provide information on choice, support studies, personal support and most importantly are around to see people. The students establish peer groups with their colleagues which tend to help support each other, through discussing assignments or problems and looking for solutions. Curriculum flexibility breaks down these support models as there is no obvious peer group and the course team becomes more dissipated.

The challenge facing institutions is to find a student support framework that creates the appropriate culture and mechanism for support. In order to achieve this the change needs to be seen positively by staff who must be reassured that it is not about throwing away all that has been well developed in the past.

This is one of the most difficult parts of the jigsaw when seeking to persuade colleagues and their managers. There are major debates within education about the need/desirability of a flexible curriculum. Many will argue that students come because they want to follow a particular course and the introduction of greater flexibility means that they have to study other things as well. The whole organizational ethos is based on the current form of course provision and people identify with their comfort zones at times of change and resist that change.

Many managers, particularly heads of department, see flexibility as interference with the departmental mission, inhibiting their control of the process and leading to a diminution of their resource base as they may lose students. In effect their power base is threatened and they will come out fighting. The arguments used will not be about resources and power; they will be presented in terms of educational coherence, what the professions want and student demand. They will ignore the argument that the current model may fit today, but does it address the needs of tomorrow's educational demands?

In this environment it is important to separate the two issues, namely guidance and learner support from the more controversial concept of curriculum flexibility. At Sheffield Hallam University the approach adopted was to propose a more flexible curriculum as a means of responding to the future educational needs to be addressed by the sector. This was fiercely debated within the university and led to periods of lively consideration of different viewpoints. The senior management was determined that greater flexibility was to be created. There was resistance from the schools in the university, initially formally and then by subterfuge. Eventually different models of flexibility were introduced as the schools were gradually 'brought into line'.

This was a very difficult time for those of us involved in the process of supporting the change, which, in my own case, was from my position as a middle-level manager with responsibility for the cross-institutional credit accumulation and transfer scheme. Everything that went wrong was blamed upon the move to flexibility and we had to take decisions on where we stood and how we could continue to push for change. We decided against pursuing the line that the institution has decided and 'you must comply'. It is much more important to take people with you. We therefore concentrated on asking colleagues how they would approach dealing with the implications of the new policies, thereby moving to a situation where they began to 'own the problem' and seek solutions.

Although some staff will always oppose such change it is interesting to watch how some of the early protagonists are now some of the most vociferous campaigners for the change. It is these people who will deliver the real change because they are arguing the case on the ground. Our role became one of facilitating and empowering these colleagues.

This was a period of blood-letting and acrimonious exchanges but once the programme planners got down to real curriculum development a lot of the barriers and hostility disappeared. Undoubtedly this was due to the time spent talking through the changes and encouraging ownership of the problems. Only then did the discussions and proposals in respect of guidance and learner support became public. A large working group was established with considerable teaching staff representation. The working group was charged with developing a guidance framework to fit a flexible curriculum. The general view from teaching staff was that this was to be positively welcomed as it lifted a burden from them and led to the student being regarded as important by the university. By having the flexibility debate out of the way, staff could see the logic behind the guidance framework and it became well supported.

By the time the final proposals (drafted by a number of colleagues and myself) went to the academic board there had already been full discussion of the interim report at all levels of the university and the proposals were effectively regarded as being agreed (Sheffield Hallam University, 1993). At the academic board only two directors of school spoke against the proposals and their argument was not about the guidance framework but an attempt to re-open the debate about curriculum flexibility.

It was a stormy journey and no doubt there will be more icebergs to come but the general acceptance by staff and support of the senior management were the key features in achieving the change.

Class size

One of the major challenges facing institutions is how to organize educational programmes and support when student numbers are rising and the unit of resource is declining. This affects all institutions and places enormous pressure on academic staff. The normal consequence of increasing student numbers is that class sizes increase. This increase though does not take place overnight. It tends to take the form of an extra student every year until suddenly the class is twice the size it used to be. Such a scenario usually means that little attention has been paid to identifying different learning and support techniques.

The pressure of work through increased marking, trying to ensure that students are all involved in the learning process and ensuring that inadequate learning resources can be further stretched mean that staff are less available to see students. It is now commonly reported that students have difficulty seeing the appropriate member of staff. In many institutions the personal tutor system has broken down as the resource has been transferred to direct teaching. However, because of the increase in class size it is the support function that needs to be further developed to enable the student to survive.

Alongside the pressure brought about by increased class size is the growing competitiveness around research and consultancy. Both of these activities take staff away from the classroom and students. These activities are important to the individual and the institution but they place further strain on the student experience as the member of staff is not as available for personal consultation. In putting forward the guidance proposals this argument was crucial in gaining support from other academic colleagues.

For years they had been struggling with the demands placed upon them by larger groups. They recognized that they did not have the time to provide the level of service they were used to and that they needed help. They identified the framework as giving them the opportunity to see a general enhancement in the support of students. Effectively they were supportive because the benefits were clear.

Student charters

The UK has attempted to introduce a culture of levels of service performance. This is known as the 'Citizens Charter' whereby the government has committed the public sector to specify expected levels of performance and give dissatisfied individuals the ability to complain and seek redress. Many of the early charters applied to the railway system (The Passengers Charter), the health service (The Patients Charter) and other front-line services. In 1993 the DfE produced Student Charters for further and higher education (DfE, 1993a, 1993b). The two charters are different in a number of ways which reflects the needs of students in the two sectors. It is interesting to note that further education colleges have to prepare their own charter for distribution to students whereas universities have no such obligation. The production of charters raises questions of service delivery and redress for the student. The charter only has any meaning if service standards are clearly spelt out and the student has a right of redress. We could all be spending the majority of our time considering complaints because the charter statement has been left suitably vague and ambiguous to ensure the institution has not left itself open to challenge.

A number of institutions had already started to address charters and statements of student entitlement prior to the Prime Minister launching the Citizens Charter concept. Many of these institutions wanted to develop statements that explained to the student the level of service they could expect and what their rights are. The importance of the charter movement is not necessarily what the charters say but that it publicly raises the issue of student satisfaction. The pressure around such a development will come from the students themselves as part of the process is their empowerment. A challenge from that group is the most difficult to resist or ignore.

In terms of influencing change and being a catalyst for that change I have found that the charter is an effective vehicle. Institutions know that they have to address the spirit as well as the letter of the charter. This presents an opportunity to push for changes on the basis that the charter requires them; this is why the charter is so important – not for what it says or does not say but the opportunity it provides to determine an enhanced student experience that matters. What we have attempted to do at Sheffield is to produce a major document indicating the rights and entitlements a student has and to match that against their responsibilities, the Partnership in Learning.

This Partnership in Learning is not based on bland charter-type statements but has tried to move on into significantly more detail. It does not prescribe to academic staff what they must deliver but, more importantly, provides the framework in which they can agree to operate. This is a crucial distinction as my experience suggests that if you provide staff with an enabling framework they will generally accept it, whereas if you are too prescriptive they are likely to oppose and ignore it. One example of this was when an early draft of the Partnership in Learning stated that assessed work should be returned to the student within four weeks of its submission with detailed comments for feedback purposes. This was not very well received and all the reasons as to why this might not work were raised. However, the compromise version which states that 'at the beginning of each module the student will be told when work has to be submitted, when it will be returned and the arrangements for feedback', was relatively well received as it provided a framework in which they could develop their own work plan. Staff see the issue as one under their control because they specify the dates and the details, accept that it is a reasonable objective but are aware that it has come about because of institutional debate about the charter. The charter reinforces the need to instil a culture change in the organization and colleagues generally agreed with more detailed specifications that actually mean something in practice.

Student services

The key agency in responding to such changes should be the section or department responsible for student services. Generally though, these departments were not set up for this purpose. The traditional role of such departments is as a 'blue flashing light' service to which the student who has a major 'problem' is referred. In many cases there is then a problem for the student in finding that service because it may not be conveniently located. The services generally tend to be of a reactive nature where 'problems' are referred rather than being a proactive service which is designed to ensure that students are fully supported.

This form of student service has begun to change, most notably in further education. It is not easy to make such changes. For many years the services have been seen as the 'Cinderella' section. They will have received little, if any, additional funding during the expansion of student numbers. Many academic staff in the teaching departments always begrudge resource going to central departments, other than the library, because they do not contribute to the 'real work of the institution'. Much of this culture has been created by resource models adopted by institutions and the trend to provide support through course teams. As we have seen the latter is breaking down as there are more students.

WHAT CHANGES ARE NEEDED?

The major change required is in the attitude of the institution. For years institutions have invested time and energy in developing strategic plans, mission statements, marketing plans, curriculum flexibility and the devolution of budgets. Comparatively little time has been allocated to the planning of student support models. There has been a general assumption that they are coping. As has been argued earlier this assumption is not well founded. In order to ensure that students are appropriately supported there needs to be a shift in attitude and in the culture of the organization. Most institutions have spent years telling students what they cannot do; little attention has been paid to advising students what they can do.

We need to place the student at the forefront of our thinking and to make sure that our practices reflect the needs of the student. We need to have a student champion who will liaise with the Students' Union and promote their concerns. In many old universities this is the role of the registrar, but of course they are also the people who make the rules about what can or cannot be done. There is in effect a need for a dean of students along the model commonly adopted in the USA.

Whether an institution decides to have such a role or not is obviously a matter for internal structures but what is required is a student-oriented framework in the institution. This framework needs to recognize that students are becoming more independent as learners and are clearer about their requirements. The framework should therefore operate on the principle of student empowerment. An empowered student is one who is equipped with the means to tackle the problem. Once we have empowered the students we will have a more questioning and demanding educational process. The important task is to ensure that the empowerment takes place. There will undoubtedly be a number of ways in which this can happen. One model is to consider the activities currently used, review them to see what is missing, then fill the gaps. To overhaul the approach though, requires the use of a change agent and that agent should pursue a proactive approach to student support.

In many cases the change in approach has been orchestrated by the institution reviewing the nature and level of student support, reviewing the role of the student service function and repositioning student services. In many colleges we have seen the development of client services, where the student and potential student are seen as clients of the organization and a customer care approach has been adopted. Many of these services are seen as a 'front of house' service which deals with general enquiries and support issues. These services work closely with teaching teams. Their importance is not just in their being able to see students but their role in pursuing change. Many teaching teams recognize the difficulties addressed earlier but because they are only part of a large organization they find it difficult to promote change. Indeed in many cases they are regarded as putting forward special pleading. The central service is much more able to promote change across the institution through identifying and then building upon good practice.

For many years the 'central' function in universities has been regarded with suspicion, bordering upon hostility by schools and departments. Much of this antagonism is a result of the central functions being seen as over-resourced and not contributing to the 'real work' of the institution. The increased productivity in the last ten years has essentially been delivered through increases in class size and therefore more work for teachers. At the same time there is a perception that the number of 'administrators' has increased. This culture makes it difficult for central services to take such a developmental role. However, it is an ideal opportunity for parts of the 'centre' to show that they have expertise in an area of work directly related to the learning process. It is imperative that the central service works closely with the teaching staff to agree a student support framework, to implement it and then to evaluate it.

But, of course, it is not only with the teaching units that tensions develop. In some cases the department of student services may also be resistant to change. Many of the staff will have been appointed on the basis of its previous role and are not comfortable with the changing environment. Indeed, many of them may well oppose the concept of curriculum flexibility. They will see the role of student services as being the department that can help when asked but are concerned about it taking a proactive approach. Consequently, when resources are allocated to develop the framework and to establish the 'change agent', there is an element of resistance and suspicion from the student services. They may see the new part as the 'Johnny and Jackie come latelies' who are getting all the resources and addressing issues in which they may have an interest. This will lead to a defensive reaction but it is important that it is recognized as people looking for safe territory and being unhappy with the marshy grounds of change management.

One way around such tensions is to develop a student support framework as part of the process of empowering the student. Many of these activities exist in all institutions but they tend to be uncoordinated and disparate. It is the role of the framework to bring them together, to ensure they are spelt out and to ensure the level and quality of the provision. It also brings together the component parts of the student service function and demonstrates to the teaching areas that the investment is worth it.

CONCLUSION

The key factor identified here for successfully managing change within a large diverse institution is to seek to take people at all levels with you. This requires a carefully thought through framework which enables staff to see the value of change.

It is not easy to secure change in an environment where staff are unused to being given clear direction and have worked in a relatively autonomous manner for years. To impose change merely increases the resistance.

The success we have achieved to date has been founded upon enhancing the student experience. This touches a particular sense of consciousness among staff to which they respond positively. The challenge is to make sure that the staff feel involved, that they are contributing to the process, that they 'own' the concept, but at the same time to play down any talk that there is a process of change taking place. It is only on reflection that people will realize the extent of the change which has taken place because they were so much part of the process.

REFERENCES

Audit Office/OFSTED (1993) *Unfinished Business,* London: HMSO.

Department for Education (1993a) *Higher Quality and Choice: The Charter for Higher Education,* London: DfE.

Department for Education (1993b) *Further Choice and Quality: The Charter for Further Education,* London: DfE.

Sheffield Hallam University (1989) *Survey into the Student Experience* (Internal Report).

Sheffield Hallam University (1993) *Final Report of the Advice and Guidance in a Flexible Institution Working Party* (Internal Report).

Robertson, D (1994), *Choosing to Change, Extending Access, Choice and Mobility in Higher Education*, London: Higher Education Quality Council.

Chapter 9

Strategic Management of the Further Education Curriculum

Ian Todd

INTRODUCTION

Like the majority of curriculum managers, my route to managerial responsibility began with a lecturing appointment. I have had the good fortune to have progressed through all of the lecturing grades and to have held appointments in institutions of both further and higher education (two further education colleges, a college of further and higher education and a former polytechnic). My subject was law. In hindsight, it is clear that this has been the single greatest influence in my approach to curriculum management. This influence has resulted, in particular, from:

- the desire of lawyers to locate particular instances within a conceptual framework;
- the willingness of lawyers to accept the problem that presents itself for solution without undue concern for the fact that the problem should not have arisen in the first place, that it is unfair that it has arisen or that a solution is not immediately discernible;
- the certainty of lawyers that, whatever the brief, the application of intellect will lead to a position being attainable which promotes the interest of the client;
- the further certainty of lawyers that there will be a number of positions which can be achieved and that each will have to be assessed to determine which should be adopted.

What follows, for good or ill, is an outline of an approach to curriculum management which reflects these influences in that it is conceptual; accepts difficult starting points without anguish; confidently expects that approaches can be fashioned which promote the interests of students provided energy is channelled into constructive thinking rather than negative and unproductive analysis and criticism; and involves constant appraisal of alternatives. As with most of the output of lawyers it will not be everyone's cup of tea!

The focus for this chapter is the identification of a strategic direction for curriculum management in the context of the broader changes outlined in Chapter 1. It is personal in that the particular direction which is outlined has been determined through an approach to management which is clearly related to a specific form of academic training and culture. It is part of that academic tradition to express thoughts in objective terms and to emphasize concepts rather than the identity or personality of the thinker. True to that tradition, this chapter places more emphasis on the strategic issues which confront curriculum managers and the solutions which emerge, than on the personal experiences of the author in implementing those solutions.

THE POLICY FRAMEWORK

Lawyers are, of course, preoccupied with rules and policy. Fortunately for this lawyer, policy has never been clearer for the curriculum manager in further education in the UK.

For years the UK has invested in a system which provides first class further and higher education to a minority of its workforce and virtually no structured, and progressive, educational opportunity to the majority. In consequence, the country has had the lowest percentage of qualified employees of the major economies. Economic competitiveness alone requires a change in this approach. The potential social benefits of up-skilling the workforce and the pool of labour from which the workforce is drawn, irrespective of social class, previous affinity for educational structures and processes or immediate employability, make the case for change irresistible.

How is government to achieve this change? It must encourage its suppliers of further and higher education to expand their provision to accommodate a much greater percentage of the potential workforce and it must provide them with funding to support this expansion. So far, so good. How much funding must it provide? This is the stage at which opinions differ, though most commentators will arrive at the same conclusion. Government has a clear choice: it can provide either sufficient funds to enable it to extrapolate the existing unit of resource (ie, the sum spent on the average full-time equivalent [FTE] student) to accommodate the larger number of citizens participating in further education, or it can provide a unit of resource for growth which is lower than that currently representing the average unit of resource. To adopt the former strategy implies either an increase in taxation or a reduction in government spending in other policy areas (eg, health, social services, pensions, primary, secondary or higher education). The adoption of the latter strategy also carries this implication but involves smaller increases in taxation or smaller cuts in other service areas. Inevitably, government is forced to conclude that a movement from an elitist to an egalitarian system of continuing education cannot be accompanied by an extrapolation of the existing unit of resource. The political costs of such a strategy would, quite simply, be unacceptable. It follows that a major growth in further education must be accommodated, in part, by efficiency savings.

THE INFLUENCE OF POLICY ON THE UNIT OF RESOURCE

The proven strategy for achieving these savings while providing incentives to institutions to seek significant growth rates, is to provide additional funding for growth but to provide such funding at a level which is lower than that represented by the existing unit of resource. This strategy leads to the interplay of two concepts:

- average cost, represented by the average existing level of funding for an FTE student, and
- marginal cost, represented by the level of funding for additional FTE students.

Where the marginal cost of educating additional students is less than the average cost of educating the existing student population, the introduction of large numbers of students at marginal cost will inexorably reduce average cost.

This can best be illustrated by reference to a particular example. If a college of further education has a budget of £6m and a student population of 3,000 FTE students its average unit of resource, and its average cost, is £2,000. So long as government is prepared to pay this college £2,000 for every additional student it enrols the average cost will remain constant and there will be no profound effect upon curriculum delivery. Should, however, the government fix its marginal unit of resource for growth, and marginal cost, at £1,500 – a relatively generous 75 per cent of average cost – the situation is transformed. A growth of 25 per cent from 3,000 FTE students to 3,750 students has the following effect:

- 3,000 FTE students attract £2,000 each, or £6m;
- 750 FTE students attract £1,500 each, or £1.125m;
- the college receives £7.125m for 3,750 FTE students;
- the new average cost, and average unit of funding, for the college is £7.125m ÷ 3,750 = £1,900.

Here is the central issue for the curriculum manager. Prior to the growth in student numbers he or she could spend £2,000 on every FTE student. Following growth the student must now be educated for £1,900.

REDUCING COSTS IN A COLLEGE

The curriculum manager is now faced with a number of choices. He or she may:

i. *Maintain the unit of resource.* This will be achieved, in the college of our example, by recruiting only the number of students who attract the 'old' (and, therefore, in the eyes of many, the 'correct') unit of resource. The effect of this will be to: reduce the college budget; require the disposal of a proportion of the college's assets to achieve savings; ensure that there is no movement to greater participation in continuing education; and indeed, reduce the number of students undertaking further post-compulsory education.

ii. *Maintain the college's student population.* This will be achieved by recruiting 3,000 FTE students. The effect of this will also be to decrease the college budget, but by less than in option (i).

iii. *Maintain the college's budget.* This will be achieved by securing £6m. To secure this sum the college will need to enrol 2,700 students at the 'old' rate and 400 students at the marginal rate. The effect of this will be to: secure the college budget of £6m; avoid any need to dispose of assets; require the college to educate an additional 100 FTE students with no additional funding; contribute an additional 100 FTE students to the pool of the vocationally educated workforce.

iv. *Go for growth.* In the example, an 8 per cent growth in student FTEs will produce an additional 240 FTE students. The effect of this will be to: increase the college's budget by £210,000; reduce the average unit of resource to just over £1,900 (from £2,000); avoid any need to dispose of assets; require the college to educate an additional 240 FTE students; contribute additional students to the pool of the vocationally educated workforce.

These figures have been provided for illustrative purposes. What is important is the principle which underlies recent mechanisms for funding teaching in further and higher education and its impact on institutions.

It will now be seen that any curriculum manager who wishes to facilitate increased access to further education and/or maintain the institution's budget must commit his or her college to growth. A minimalist approach to this task will result in the manager having no additional resources to fund the growth. Only by committing the college to significant growth does the manager promote access, secure the college's budget and receive additional resources to fund the additional students.

THE CURRICULUM IMPLICATIONS OF SIGNIFICANT GROWTH

The curriculum manager in a college which has concluded that it must commit itself to significant growth will find that the college can no longer afford to deliver its curriculum in the way it has previously been delivered. What is to be done about this? The options are clear:

a. The college's staff can take a pay cut.
b. The college can alter the conditions of service of its academic staff so that they are required to teach more hours per week or more weeks per year, or both, so that it can teach the increased number of students with no increase in staffing.
c. The college can retain the pay and conditions of service of its staff and change the way in which it delivers the curriculum so that its costs can now be accommodated by the new unit of resource.

When managing curriculum delivery in an environment of a declining unit of resource the manager can either, therefore, seek to reduce staffing costs by addressing (attacking!) the pay and conditions of service of individual staff or, seek to reduce costs by the adoption of new forms of curriculum delivery.

If the decline in the unit of resource is likely to be part of a continuum it is difficult to see how the former strategy can operate in the long term. Is there to be a modification of pay and/or conditions of service every time an increase in student numbers reduces the average level of funding? If so, the enthusiasm of the staff for increased access to post-16 continuing education is likely to wane and the manager is likely to find it increasingly difficult to point to the rewards which accompany increased productivity.

In the long term, therefore, the fundamental issues which relate to increased access can only be addressed through continuing modification of curriculum delivery models. This is the only approach which brings together the long-term interests of government, potential recipients of continuing education, colleges and their staff.

CHANGING CURRICULUM DELIVERY TO ACCOMMODATE INCREASED ACCESS

At the most basic level of analysis there are only three ways in which a college can reduce its costs by changing the way in which it delivers the curriculum. It can:

1. reduce staffing costs (the largest cost, by far, in any college) by reducing the number of hours that lecturers meet students (class contact);
2. increase the size of the classes allocated to its lecturers; or
3. effect a combination of 1 and 2 above.

The theoretical framework is clear. The practical consequences of adopting the framework are, however, so profound as to create a bewildering agenda of change for the curriculum manager. What is this agenda and how does it arise? Some of the key implications of options 1 and 2 are considered below.

1. Reduction of lecturer contact hours

Any strategy which involves the reduction of lecturer contact hours confronts a basic tenet of the culture of further education. For many staff a course is, quite simply, the aggregate of the class contact hours allocated to lecturers. A reduction in class contact hours is seen, therefore, as a decrease in course time and as a negative factor in relation to the achievement of quality.

This attitude is genuinely held and vigorously advanced. It is, however, only possible to advance this point of view if it is demonstrable that *all* encounters between students and staff are of a higher order, in promoting learning, than other forms of learning; and if it can be shown that *all* encounters between students and staff are of optimum quality in that students, as well as staff, have pre-planned the encounter so as to derive maximum advantage from this use of scarce resources. This burden of proof, it is suggested, is one which cannot be discharged. If so it follows that it is not possible to establish a causal relationship between the aggregate of course hours and learning achievement.

Quite clearly, however, any curriculum plan which offers no structured learning in lieu of class contact hours which have been withdrawn must involve a loss of learning opportunity to the student. There is a seductive simplicity in the view that cost-effective curriculum delivery can be achieved by reducing course hours, curtailing the student entitlement to access college resources and, perhaps, deliver two academic programmes with the same resource mix of lecturers, rooms and equipment that previously delivered one programme. This, however, is the way to disaster. A reduction of class contact hours must not be seen as involving a reduction in course hours and there must exist a strategic plan for replacing one learning opportunity with another.

At Newcastle College there has been a major investment programme in learning resources and a considerable base has been established for library-based study and for the provision of IT facilities outside of class contact. Despite this investment, however, it is clear that two problems remain. In the first place, library-based study is, for most students, not an adequate replacement for class contact if it is not planned and integrated into a coherent programme of learning experiences.

Second, in some courses (eg, construction crafts, hairdressing, catering) there is a limit to the contribution that library study can reasonably be expected to make to the achievement of the students' learning objectives. These problems can only be tackled by:

- ensuring that a coherent curriculum model exists for all courses which plans the relationship between lectures, library-based study, small group activity and other forms of learning to ensure that the library-based activities of the students build upon the platform established by lecturers in class contact and are, in turn, supported by small group activities through which students receive feedback in relation to the tasks undertaken in the library;
- developing a strategy for learning outside of class contact which acknowledges that physical areas must be created and staffed to enable students to practise their skill development in a safe and supportive environment.

The college has been successful in some areas in developing a culture which acknowledges that the student must operate within a work schedule (or curriculum plan) which integrates the various components of their learning, but has not yet been able to achieve a college-wide adoption of comprehensive curriculum planning. It is only at the early stages of its thinking in relation to the provision of a practical focus for non-class contact study for craft courses.

The reduction of lecturer contact hours is an essential component of any comprehensive strategy for coping with growth at a marginal unit of resource which is significantly lower than the average unit. It does not, however, produce savings which can be immediately deployed in support of newly introduced or newly extended learning programmes, for some considerable part of the savings must be reinvested to create an appropriate and adequately resourced learning environment. Moreover, if a college's learning culture does not change, the redistribution of resources to support non-contact student learning will probably not result in a return on capital which matches the efficiency and effectiveness of the lecturer contact which has been surrendered.

For the curriculum manager the agenda for action which results from the conclusion that a reduction in class contact is inevitable includes the following:

- How should the college's physical resources be reconfigured to accommodate the learning needs of the students released from the classroom?
- What are the equipment and learning materials (eg, books, learning packages, software, video) requirements of the staff responsible for managing the newly developed learning areas?
- How are course teams to be encouraged to plan a whole week learning experience for full-time students and a whole day learning experience for part-time students?

The agenda is daunting. However, there is evidence to demonstrate that when a strategic curriculum movement within a college coincides with a course team's willingness to plan a coherent and comprehensive learning experience for students which integrates learning inside and outside the classroom, there is a step change in quality which is brought about as a simple result of the degree of thought and preparation that has been given to the curriculum plan. At Newcastle College the evidence includes the following.

a. The students' perception of the value of an encounter with lecturers can be influenced by the rationing of this entitlement.

In one area of work within the college, that of office studies, the lecturing staff were faced with inordinate pressure resulting from the introduction of national vocational qualifications (NVQs). This pressure took the form of a continual demand from students for contact with their lecturers, typically for guidance in relation to assessment or for the actual process of assessment. This pressure was only relieved by the introduction of a defined entitlement to contact with the lecturer which was given a physical manifestation by the introduction of a credit card (the credit being an allocation of time). The effect of the introduction of this card was profound. The immediate effect was to discipline students so that they came to see their time with lecturers for what it is, the consumption of a scare resource. Students became reluctant to use any part of their credit allocation until they had planned the encounter so as to make it as profitable as possible. The card thus promoted pre-planning. In time, students came to realise that they had concerns which were common and began to understand that they could share their entitlement by meeting with staff in groups rather than as individuals. In effect students were accepting a higher student staff ratio (SSR) in their encounters with staff in order to maximise the number of encounters. Further, the peer group discussion which became part of the planning of such encounters became a learning experience in its own right. Virtually all these outcomes were unplanned and, in effect, a bonus to staff who would never have been able to predict the consequences of their planning.

b. Students are eager to practise machine-based activities in time allocated to them for learning outside of class contact.

In some subjects students are introduced to processes (eg, keyboarding) or to software which they need to practise. In most of these cases it is implausible to argue that the practice cannot take place effectively outside of class contact. The evidence of the college is that every machine-based facility it opens in support of such students outside of class contact is filled to capacity within an extremely short timescale. It is, moreover, filled by students who are visibly undertaking their studies with an eagerness and sense of purpose.

The demand for such facilities is increasingly coming from students who are not students of IT, *per se,* but have been asked to word-process essays, assignments or projects.

c. Students are eager to practise their skills through other forms of learning technology.

Not all students wish to devote significant periods of time to machine-based learning. They will, however, be drawn with equal interest and enthusiasm to other forms of learning technology. The college has, for example, created a maths workshop supported by learning materials. These materials lead the student, through initial diagnosis, worked examples and structured feedback, to the achievement of specified learning objectives. The materials were originally acquired by the college for use during class contact. Increasingly, however, the demand upon them is made by 'drop-in' students utilizing their non-contact learning time to reinforce their skills.

d. Students respond to opportunities to access technology to enhance their projects, assignments or portfolios.

The introduction by Newcastle College of new technology in support of non-class contact activity by students has invariably created a demand which is larger than the initially determined supply. This is the case whether the technology is complex (as with video production) or simple (eg, a colour photocopier). It is clear that students value access to resources which enable them to produce high quality copy for work which is to be undertaken outside of class contact but which is to be formally assessed. If the assessment is external to the organization the value placed by students on access to such facilities intensifies.

The process of assembling the copy to be assessed is, typically, one which involves the student operating, without direct supervision by lecturers, in a focused and organized manner. The output is frequently of outstanding quality.

2. Increasing class size

Increases in class size are invariably seen by a number of stakeholders (lecturers, students, parents and employers) as an indication of deteriorating quality. This belief is so firmly rooted in the value systems of some stakeholders that they are, quite simply, not prepared to debate the issue.

Where this is the case, the belief that increases in class size will undermine the quality of curriculum delivery is likely to become self-fulfilling. A reduction in quality is almost certain if increases in class size are not matched by changes in the model for curriculum delivery. Large classes cannot be taught as though they were small classes. If a course with, say, 15 hours of class contact is assumed to have 20–30 students and the full cohort of students is assumed to be present at every meeting of the class, an adjustment in class size to 60–70 is likely to have a profound effect. The opportunity for individuals to participate in class discussion is significantly diminished, lecturers have fewer opportunities to provide students with feedback in relation to classwork or homework and the burden of marking is likely to lead to lecturers setting less work for students to complete. Students find it more difficult to make personal contact with their lecturers and their fellow students and can become disenchanted with their studies. A failure to provide a room which is large enough to contain the expanded group without a need to 'raid' adjacent rooms for chairs or for students to sit on tables or the floor greatly exacerbates this sense of unease and creates an environment in which lecturers and students feel that there is no plan and no order. If there has been no change in curriculum planning they will, of course, be correct. Without a new curriculum plan a manager will not be able to provide a new environment and a vicious downward spiral of quality will ensue.

To break out of this spiral or, better still, to prevent it arising, an increase in class size requires a major commitment from managers and lecturers. The starting point for this commitment is the curriculum delivery model. When devising a new model it is often difficult not to merely tinker with the existing model, but this must be avoided at all costs. Moreover, the model must be logically consistent. If it is argued that a class of 60–70 is too large for interaction (and there are those who would dispute this assumption) then why should the class not grow to 80, 90 or 100? If 100 why not 150 or 200? The creation of such super-large classes will create significant opportunities for small groups and can create not only a more efficient delivery model than that which supported the group of 20–30 but also a more effective one.

However, the curriculum manager who introduces larger classes as a response to a declining unit of resource has taken on board a number of complex and time-consuming issues. First there is the need for an appropriate physical environment. Then, there is the need to develop a curriculum delivery model for the course that now exists and to abandon the model which is now redundant. This latter task is by far the more difficult of the two.

An additional factor for the curriculum manager to consider when addressing the issue of large classes is the homogeneous nature of the class. The further education curriculum is heavily dependent upon oral delivery of subject matter by the lecturer. How, then, can a large class be assembled when the class is not homogeneous and the students wish to focus on different aspects of the same subject or on different subjects? It follows that, without such planning large classes can only be part of a curriculum delivery strategy if, by chance, a large number of students present themselves to the college to study the same subject over the same period of time.

If, however, a college elects to focus upon the *process* of learning rather than upon the subject matter it will find that it has other options. Large classes can be brought together if the organizing principle for the class is that they are all undertaking the *same process* (eg, learning from learning packages or interacting with computer packages) rather than listening to the same message orally conveyed by the lecturer. At Newcastle College a very large commitment has been made to establishing the infrastructure to enable this to happen. Thus, for example:

- seven learning resource workshops have been created to enable groups of up to 70 or, in some cases, 100 students to study from learning packages and other written material;
- non-teaching staff have been appointed to support teachers in this learning environment;
- a production capacity for learning materials has been created which involves specialist assistance with design and editing and with physical production of both original material and copies for class use;
- a very large IT suite has been created for the teaching of basic IT skills.

CONCLUSION

It is easy to represent the consequence of an expansion of further education in exclusively negative terms. The reasons for this are straightforward: the expansion involves a declining unit of resource and, because of this, either a worsening in the pay and conditions of academic staff or, if pay and conditions are to be maintained, reductions in class contact and increases in class size.

Without effective curriculum management this negative analysis will invariably prove to be correct. This then leads to a clear choice for policy makers. Either expansion of the service has to be abandoned and access to continuing education denied to large numbers of citizens, or expansion continues and the quality of continuing education deteriorates. Each of these outcomes has, of course, profound and negative social and economic effects.

Herein lies the responsibility of curriculum managers at all levels. Only the management staff of colleges can assemble the financial base and the strategy required to provide the learning environment appropriate to curriculum delivery involving less class contact and larger classes than have been traditionally represented in the further education delivery model. Only lecturers can devise and implement coherent curriculum models which integrate all forms of student learning. Unless these professional curriculum managers deploy their expertise consistently and imaginatively, society will not experience the benefits it is entitled to receive from the further education service.

PART FOUR:

OPPORTUNITIES FOR NEW ACTORS IN TIMES OF CHANGE

EDITORIAL COMMENT

The final two chapters illustrate how times of change can throw up opportunities for 'new actors' to play a role in the development of future and higher education. Lesley Cooke reflects on her transition from an enthusiastic but, as she describes it, a 'politically and institutionally naive lecturer', to taking on the role of assistant dean with the brief of stimulating and implementing change in a variety of areas across her institution. She relates how from her initial position as someone who was sceptical about the Enterprise in Higher Education (EHE) initiative she became an enthusiastic advocate. She learnt from the three strategies used to persuade her, namely, creating 'ownership', the use of persuasive advocates and the prospect of additional resources. From her initial contact with EHE, she subsequently began to attempt to initiate broader changes in areas such as compacts with local schools and colleges, promoting access for disabled students and introducing records of achievement. She reflects on the question of whether she was in fact primarily 'an agent of change' or a 'product of change', as so much of her work was part of her own staff development process.

The final word in this volume is given to a student representative. While other contributors in one way or another reflect on moral dilemmas which they have faced in conducting their roles, it is probably fair to say that Lee Whitehead does this in the most compelling manner of all! Rather than adopting a stereotypical Students' Union opposition role, when offered the opportunity to make a serious contribution to his university's strategic planning process, as president of the Students' Union he, equally seriously, accepted the invitation – following intensive soul-searching. As with all the other examples of change contained within this volume, a key strategy involved obtaining ownership by very diverse students of the proposals being put forward. Considerable time, energy and commitment were invested in bringing together groups of students to thrash out the basic principles and substance of the plan. The focus of this plan was 'the quality of the whole student experience'. The value of this process is illustrated by the new productive partnership which emerged between the university and the Students' Union.

Chapter 10

Times of Change or Times of Chance?

Lesley Cooke

INTRODUCTION

Picture yourself walking into a senior common-room and looking around you. Your initial perceptions are of a dark, high-ceilinged and smoky room. The heavy chairs, filled by elderly men in dark suits, are pulled around in inward facing circles. During that first week you listen to a debate on whether any individuals, other than academic lecturers, should be allowed into this SCR. You watch as it is decided, by vote, that only senior members of administration might be invited to use the facility. Coffee will only be available at the coffee, lunch and tea breaks, during which time the entire college will stop for the designated time period.

Picture yourself, ten years later, walking into a changed room: one now called the common-room. Still high-ceilinged, it has been redecorated and is much more brightly lit. Virtually smoke-free, it now contains a greatly increased number of chairs. These are being used by a much wider range of people: men and women, all ages; dressed in every conceivable formal and informal fashion, and representing the range of college work roles from maintenance staff to principal. Coffee is now available throughout the day, reflecting the 12-hour pattern of timetabling.

This vignette represents changes at a number of levels: changes in which I have increasingly come to play a part. Change is a pervasive phenomenon and the effects of even relatively minor changes in policy and attitude can appear in many guises. It could be argued that the character of this meeting room at the heart of the college may well be an institutional barometer, and that it measures not only the impact and impetus of past and ongoing change, but gives an indication of the dynamic of continuing and accelerating change.

Over ten years ago I came to Chester College as an enthusiastic, albeit politically and institutionally naive, psychology/sports psychology lecturer. Two years ago I was appointed to the post of assistant dean of academic studies (a 'training post' established not only as part of the college response to new contractual demands and responsibilities but also in response to the needs of an overburdened dean of academic studies). I am involved with access, admissions, student progress and development, curriculum changes, administration and management projects and initiatives, and a range of other activities in and beyond college. Next year the results of this training will be put to the test when I take up a new post as director of student guidance and support services.

The position of an assistant dean is an interesting one. I am not a senior manager, I do not have a role in the senior management team. I do not have a budget, I do not have executive authority. Yet in the two years that I have worked in this position, I have found myself increasingly contributing to strategy and change.

As I have carried out my responsibilities they have become increasingly interrelated, forming a coherent whole rather than a portfolio of different tasks. The attitude of my colleagues has changed over the last two years. It appears that I am perceived less as an assistant and more as a deputy; interpreting, explaining and serving as a sounding-board for their ideas. This is partly a reflection of the trust and responsibility placed explicitly and implicitly on me by my line manager, the dean of academic studies. It is also the result of my increasing confidence, and resulting ability to take initiative. Where does this change lie? In me or my colleagues? Or is it a product of some broader change affecting the nature of further and higher education?

The story of change at Chester is intertwined with my own story; my own shift from 'outsider' to agent of change. Because my move into management is recent and still ongoing, I write in a dual capacity: that of being changed and also of being a facilitator of change. In this chapter I identify and reflect on some of the major developmental points which occurred at Chester, and how they have contributed to my own development.

BACKGROUND

I came from pupil experience of state and direct grant schools; student experience of a specialist teacher training college (Bedford College of Physical Education), and the Universities of Cambridge and Leeds; and (after two years of school teaching) teaching/research experience within three universities and a college. Although I had received an excellent professional training in teaching and pupil management skills at Bedford, I had had no preparation for teaching in higher education. However, in these institutions I was fortunate to work with people who were prepared to help me learn 'on the job', who lent me course/lecture outlines and who were generous in giving me advice about the running of seminars and tutorials. I found that I enjoyed this work and decided that I wanted to stay in lecturing. Unfortunately though, I had entered higher education at a time when institutions were beginning to look for financial savings and for whom short-term, part-time contracts offered a way of dealing with current and potential financial constraints.

Thus I came to Chester with experience of frozen posts, short-term contracts, part-time work and a general experience of uncertainty and doubt about the future, but also possessing a wide experience of a range of different types of educational institutions. This experience, however, was all earned at the interface; I had always been the student or the lecturer. I was completely naive about the way in which higher education institutions were managed. I had no experience or understanding of structure or procedures, nor any desire so to do. Previous contracts had focused on teaching or research, not on any commitment to the overall functioning of the institution. I perceived myself as a researcher/teacher/lecturer and wanted to do this and this only. Chester seemed to offer me the opportunity to teach, to work with students and colleagues in the academic context, and most important of all Chester seemed to offer stability in a changing world. Now, as assistant dean I have little opportunity to do teaching or research. Flexibility rather than stability underpins my work, and I find I enjoy the challenge of development and change.

What follows reflects my perceptions of what occurred and is occurring at one particular institution. The 'accuracy' of perceptions are rooted in the individual's experience and interpretation of events. As I have learned more about educational policy and practice, about management, strategy and delivery, my interpretations of what I see, hear and read have changed in quality and complexity. My perceptions may still be at variance with the intentions of senior management, but I suspect that there is greater congruity than ever before. Whether I became assistant dean because of this increasing congruity or whether the congruity is a result of 'assisting' is a moot point. Perhaps the most important thing to recognize is that I believe that total congruity in perceptions (besides being an impossibility) would serve to detract from my value as a change agent and as a member of the college.

EDUCATIONAL VALUES AND VISIONS

Chester College was founded in 1839 as Chester Diocesan Training College. Bradbury (1975) describes how the 'weight of those behind the founding of the College were Tory in politics as well as Church in religion'. One of the founders, Lord Stanley, urged that the function of the college was to bring 'the best of the Church's spiritual and academic gifts to bear, even if indirectly...on the masses of the deprived in the great new cities' and, according to Bradbury's History of the College, he served warning of the dangers of doing nothing in an ivory tower (pp. 52–5).

The original aims were to provide:

- an elementary school for the children of the poor to be regarded as a model school;
- a school for the education of masters of elementary schools for the children of the poor;
- a middle school for the education of the children of the middle classes (standing as a subsidiary objective).

It is interesting to consider these aims in the current context:

- the original model 'day school' has long been turned to other uses. But a new 'primary base' has been built to provide the space and equipment necessary for student teachers to practise their skills on children brought in from local schools (including a fair number of 'children of the poor');
- the college had moved from the notion of training 'masters for elementary schools' through the rise, decline and re-emergence of secondary teacher training; the advent of women students; the introduction of BEd, BA and BSc degree

programmes; the development of primary and secondary (postgraduate) teacher training; and a broad development of in-service and postgraduate degrees. Today, in common with all departments engaged in professional studies, it faces the challenge of yet more change.

The educational aims and vision of the college today are clearly delineated in the mission statement: although language and context has changed, the vision can be seen as constant. The college seeks, *inter alia*, to:

- facilitate a widening of access to higher education within the local community;
- collaborate with employers in preparing students to make a positive contribution in the social and economic context;
- offer all students, through the work of its ecumenical chaplaincy, opportunities to give systematic consideration to the personal and social challenges of Christian teachings.

So where do I fit in this? As an individual, I find that my personal beliefs fit with the underlying principles of the college mission: community, increased access, greater equality of opportunity, maintenance of quality and the striving for excellence. Bound up in the perceptions of the 'ordinary lecturer' it took me a while to realize this. For several years I was so burdened by the 'new lecturer's' role and so intimidated by my seniors that I didn't have space, opportunity or desire to reflect on the broader institution. However, colleagues gave me support which underpinned early steps in confidence, and I am pleased that these people have continued as mentors and friends since those first days. Today, there is a formalization of this support; through staff induction procedures. Although individuals may still perceive themselves as struggling with the problems of teaching and marking, there is greater understanding of the nature and content of the support that the new lecturer sees as relevant. New staff are encouraged to take the opportunity to establish formal as well as informal mentoring arrangements, facilitating the ease with which they become part of our community. Later in this chapter I will return to this notion of 'community', not only because it is a fundamental part of our lives in further and higher education, but also because it has the power to be either the facilitator or the impediment to change, irrespective of the change agent!

TURNING POINTS

A sequence of events occurred between 1987 and 1992 which had considerable impact on the college development yet which, arguably, have taken us closer to the original mission of the college. In 1987 a new principal was appointed who capitalized on the opportunities offered by the governmental changes in education policy to encourage development and change in the college. In 1989 Chester was awarded funding in the second round of Enterprise in Higher Education (EHE), stimulating and supporting change in curriculum and delivery. A new deputy principal was appointed in 1992 and despite precipitating a degree of two-way culture shock, this has successfully resolved itself into a stimulating and challenging partnership. Linked with these events were a number of developments including the senior management team decision to increase the staff:student ratio from 14.5:1 to 20:1 and to increase expenditure on learning resources and staff development.

As Chapter 1 of this volume has indicated, the EHE initiative was designed to encourage qualities of confidence, capability and enterprise in the undergraduate population. It takes the form of a three-way relationship between employers , academic staff and students. Today, the college is recognized as a successful example of institutional commitment and integration of enterprise in higher education. Initially however, for most of us, the notion of 'enterprise' was anathema, analogous to entrepreneurship and 'riding roughshod' over others. We experienced considerable disquiet with the idea of 'wealth creation' as a desirable characteristic in students, and initially perceived EHE to be at variance with the educational and political tenets of the college. Indeed, for some, the perceived political underpinnings of the scheme still continue to hinder their commitment to the projects that evolve from the funding, even though it has become increasingly clear that the student experience is enhanced. However, mainly because of the positive results with the students, staff came to terms with the 'characteristics'. They recognized that there was a much closer relationship between these and those aspects normally deemed 'academic' than originally believed, notably the ability to communicate ideas, work in a team, work towards excellence and to work to deadlines.

For me, EHE was to provide a unique stimulus for change when it funded my attendance at a Department for Education conference at which staff from Alverno College (Milwaukee, USA) were presenting an overview of their philosophy and practice. Visits to Alverno over the next few years gave me opportunity to see, take part in and reflect on their work. On return to Chester, I was encouraged by senior management to communicate my learning through contributing to staff development. Additionally I was given my first college-wide responsibility, that of negotiating an exchange agreement with Alverno. These initial steps laid the path to my current position and the responsibilities that go with it.

Reflecting on the EHE adventure, it becomes clear that if people undertake and then articulate a new task or role, they are more likely to become supporters in future. It is the subtle balance of push and pull that makes for good management of change. Thus when we, as staff, were first introduced to EHE,

- we were encouraged to take part in open debate, filling *our* need to feel part of the decision-making process (even though any decisions had already been made in all probability!);
- the chaplaincy team, a respected ecumenical group of colleagues, produced a report arguing that EHE could be used for good or bad, depending on how we delivered it (thus appealing to our professional pride and meeting some of our concerns about principles);
- funding was put into the first round of projects (thus giving us resources to try out the new teaching and learning methods that were to prove vital in handling the worsening staff:student ratio).

These three actions are sound strategies for the introduction of change – perceived ownership, use of 'powerful' or persuasive advocates, and funding. I endeavour to use all these in my current work, although having no budget I find that I need to use various strategies to tap into other people's financial resources.

CHANGE AGENT?

At what point did I consciously become a change agent? On reflection, I realize that as a lecturer I had been facilitating change in students for many years: changes in understanding, interpretation and presentation. But it was during this EHE and Alverno period that I began to attempt to initiate broader changes which impacted on my colleagues. Since being appointed to my current post, I have been involved in a range of activities that require me to introduce and facilitate change with both staff and students. Some have been successful, some not so! Here I focus on three particular examples which illustrate my role as change agent, but also illustrate how I myself have been changed through the opportunities that have arisen.

Compacts

A compact is the formal statement of a special relationship set up with a selected school or college, whereby access to further study at a university or advanced college is facilitated if particular pre-entry criteria are met. Such criteria might include provision of competence in study skills. Initially I was required to take over and complete one partly-developed compact. Now I have responsibility for overseeing the development of all compacts with other institutions, and have been able to initiate further compact arrangements with other individuals or groups who might benefit from facilitated access to college. This is not entirely altruistic because it has benefit for us too, for example by accessing more potential students in areas of shortage such as science.

Through this work I have learned that if I present an argument or development that has obvious benefit to colleagues, I can 'tag on' something else that might not have such easy acceptance. Additionally, I have learned that facilitating change in others is in itself a personal development issue. I now find myself in the situation of encouraging colleagues to develop compacts for their particular academic subjects/areas. I am learning that while I do not have to do the entire task, I do need to circulate information, encourage individuals, clarify the limits on their negotiations and check their paperwork. I enjoy seeing colleagues gaining confidence in themselves as external negotiators and gaining experience of the positive aspect of doing something that they (and I) believe is appropriate to our mission.

Access for disabled students

As a lecturer I found considerable opposition to the notion of having disabled sportsmen, sportswomen and students on site. Although it was possible to bring children with disability into occasional sports sessions there was no provision or support for any greater commitment.

The main argument was that Chester College, built on a multi-stepped site, is not an easy place for those with movement disability; a fact which could not be disputed at that time. Yet today we have an integrated campus, ramps and access, hearing loops and a flourishing cohort of students (hearing and hearing impaired) able and willing to use British Sign Language.

What brought about change? On reflection I see that it came about through the integration of a number of initiatives and through the work of different individuals. My role in the change dynamic was to use a mixture of behaviours: ignoring past practice, establishing precedent, using EHE funding to support a module on adapted sport, motivating the student body to support change, utilizing the support of a positively focused academic staff and students, and recognizing and using internal and external networks of experienced individuals for additional support.

It was relatively easy to initiate and run an 'adapted sport' module through the EHE initiative, and with the students' active support I was able to contribute to the creation and running of the Chester Sports Club for people with disability. Hosting the club at college at weekends allowed students to drop in to participate and coach. In what was then a rampless college, the recreation department arranged the building of a concrete access ramp to the swimming pool. Funding from the Students' Union supported the students as they began to travel to national sports events and to develop networks in the community. I found that having supported the students for the first year, by teaching them, driving them to venues and encouraging them to develop their own skills and confidence, they then became self-motivated. They set up their own support groups, obtained funding from the Union and took up opportunities to acquire teaching and coaching qualifications in disabled/adapted sports.

Facilitating the acceptance of our first profoundly deaf student was not difficult although it was a big step – a willing and interested head of department and the student's own charisma and experience were sufficient. However, the problems encountered in maintaining this change were several. Staff declared their commitment to the notion of equality of opportunity, but varied in their interpretation of this. The student herself undertook the staff and student deaf awareness training, initiated Sign Language classes and generally helped us all towards a new understanding of being disabled in an able-bodied world.

Reflecting on this change, I have learned that it is easy to build on the strengths that are already present (eg, the academic and administrative staff already committed to the notion of equal opportunity); that it is possible to introduce skills and knowledge that intrigue and interest (eg, signing skills), but that problems arise when overloaded staff who will have difficulty dealing with anything that they perceive as additional demand, are faced with change. Clearly, several staff who were working with students with special needs experienced dissonance between maintaining their belief in equality and in meeting the demands that actioning such a belief laid upon them. I believe that this made the burden of extra work seem even more onerous. As a steady trickle of deaf students begins to come to Chester, the need to establish a specific student support system becomes more immediate. The strength of a supportive Students' Union is invaluable as is the commitment of senior management and administration; without these the initiation of change would be much harder. But change cannot be embedded until an infrastructure of support is established across the institution, using academic staff, students and support staff appropriately. The lesson I learned is that ideals and beliefs can engender a charisma that initiates change, however difficult the circumstances. But I have also learned that such change is not genuine unless it can continue without the charismatic or enthusing initiator. Part of managing change is to strike the balance between inspiration and solid support.

Records of achievement

Here my perception of myself as an agent of change is endangered! As part of the EHE Initiative and student induction procedures, incoming students were required to contribute to the design of a record of achievement which they would find interesting and appropriate to use throughout their college career. With my personal tutorial group, I led a successful pilot study with particular emphasis on the document's use as a recording, reflective and action-planning device. This year the college issued all incoming first years with a revised version of this record of achievement. Staff training and staff induction dealt with issues about the use of records by staff, although emphasis was put on the fact that it was a student record to be kept by the student. Although the end-of-year evaluation still has to take place, there is anecdotal evidence that some of the staff have abdicated all responsibility for supporting the student use of the document. Some staff perceive it as additional work, and do not appear to hear any argument about the document actually being the student's responsibility. Others have taken 'student responsibility' to mean no staff commitment. Yet where the record is being developed cooperatively by staff and student, it appears to be successful.

Through this initiative I have learned that even when a strategy is well planned, successful delivery still depends on individual perceptions and commitment. In order to support the acceptance and use of the record I have used a range of resources including student enterprise, student representatives (trained to liaise between staff and the student body), selected staff, and individual 'powerful' students. But it is clear that if staff are not convinced or do not wish to pursue an initiative, then the students can pick up and act (or fail to) on the negative message. With hindsight I realize that my thrust at present must be to get the students to understand the importance and value of the record to their reflective learning, action planning and future development, both academic and in the world of employment. I want to ensure that *they* provide the 'push' which is necessary if all staff are to recognize the worth of the document and the processes it develops.

AGENT OF CHANGE OR PRODUCT OF CHANGE?

In common with many other institutions, over the past decade my own has changed in size and function. Attracting an increasingly diverse staff and student population, it has broadened its range of courses and opportunities and has become interlinked with the wider community and the world of work. In recent years I have consciously acted as an agent of change in these developments, and I have enjoyed the challenge that this creates. But on reflection, I think that some of the things I did without preplanning in past years have also contributed to, or reflected, some of the winds of change which have blown through the institution.

For example, attitudes towards dress have changed. In traditional teacher training contexts, dress was always required to be 'professional': casual dress meant casual attitude or behaviour. My refusal to accept this dictum except when on college business, my refusal to wear prescribed clothes (or my preference for those proscribed) certainly delayed some people's recognition of me as professionally competent. It also caused a lot of unnecessary comment, and even a 'telling off' or two. But those who did recognize my strengths and abilities challenged this notion, either implicitly or explicitly, recognizing what was of greater or lesser importance and worth. In the age of the universal Doc Martens boot, this might now seem an academic argument but I believe that it reflects a significant change in attitude, tolerance and a broader understanding of higher education and its concerns.

Today, staff development policies and practices attempt to make positive use of untapped energies and skills. Implementation of the college mission statement encourages work in the local and national community. A decade ago the situation was different. I was frustrated by perceived constraints. There appeared to be no development opportunities, no new courses to write or programmes to create, no teaching opportunities apart from giving lectures to 18-year-olds between 9am and 5pm. This led me to accept an opportunity outside college. I was asked to undertake some evening teaching at the local college of further education. For several years, I taught a General Certificate of Education O/A level evening class to a group of women who initially saw themselves 'only' as wives and mothers rather than intelligent individuals with family commitments. This gave me the opportunity to see the real power of education: watching them gain extraordinary confidence through study and, over more recent years, seeing them working through degree programmes with great success.

The relationship between being an agent of change, being part of change and being changed is a complex and interesting one. External influences add an extra dimension to any development in this relationship. For example; this chapter has shown how change at Chester created opportunities for me as an 'outsider' to become more fully integrated into the community and to become a change agent myself. Some of the changes that occurred opened up new opportunities, outside the established formal management hierarchies. My 'training post' was one such opportunity, and typically it has attracted someone that might not have 'dared' apply for a more conventional post. Listening to colleagues in other institutions, I understand that women are more likely to apply for such posts. The reasons for this are well-rehearsed: a complex of career breaks, family commitments and a lack of self-belief have, conventionally, held women back from applying for management positions. Short-term, sideways steps or 'small steps' into management would appear to attract such candidates. For senior management teams, this offers a way to tap into a pool of talent and creativity that might otherwise not be fully exploited. However, one question that must be addressed is that of what will happen to those individuals who show that they are ready for a greater challenge or responsibility? Will the institution be able to offer opportunities to fulfil these needs within mainstream management procedures?

Becoming a change agent is an exciting and challenging experience. Reflecting on my experiences over the past few years, I realize that I am moving from the tenets to which my early schooling and professional training introduced me to an altered set, albeit with the same underlying principles. For example, the value of striving for excellence is not questioned, but I now realize that excellence is not necessarily achieved by always doing the work myself.

A second example could focus on the powerful sense of respect for authority that my own education and training inculcated and then transmuted into an overly-defined sense of hierarchy, at which I was at the lower end. Thus one important lesson which I have learned and am still learning, is not to be afraid of others, not to allow preconceptions to hinder communication, not to assume that powerful people are 'right' by virtue of their position, and not to fear confrontation. While I recognize that hier-archy can create and maintain power sources, I have learned from experience that one can gain or be ascribed considerable power without being part of that hierarchy. Such 'power' differs in quality from the hierarchical power because there are no official sanctions to support it. But this in itself can make it stronger, because the power is given by those who choose to respect it.

Before I became assistant dean my naivety (probably a form of egocentric protection) meant that I failed to recognize that my colleagues, even those more experienced and powerful individuals, also need psychological support. I realize that I tended to differentiate people at college into three categories: lecturers/administrators/managers (who are skilled, confident and coping); friends (who might need support at particular times); and 'learners' (students and new lecturers who need positive reinforcement and support). Recent changes have put us all into the position of becoming learners, and I have come to realize that the skills and techniques of teaching and managing students and external clients are just as appropriate for managing staff.

I have had to learn to discard a lifetime belief that hard work *per se* brings success, now recognizing that the 'reward' of change does not necessarily come about just because one has employed maximum effort. The successful implementation of change depends on the development of sound strategy, recognition and resolution of problem areas, utilization of resources and ability to act flexibly. It comes about through trusting others to produce quality ideas and material that can help change occur.

I thoroughly enjoy working in a team and have had the positive experience of working successfully with colleagues and students. But I recognize that being at ease with other team members is not always the experience of others. If staff, who are already feeling threatened by change, are required to work with others with whom they do not feel comfortable, they can cause problems and difficulties, thus deliberately or accidentally blocking progress. Although I might feel apprehensive about a particular situation, it is now part of my responsibility as initiator of change to focus on supporting my colleagues, encouraging them to express and explore their fears rather than relying on being supported myself.

The concept of networking was new to me until recently. I have begun to work within a number of informal and formal networks, overcoming a fear that actively using such networks might be an unethical manipulation of friendships. I have found the process personally rewarding, interesting and very useful as I have begun to deal with the principles and practice of management.

SUMMARY

Reflecting on the transition from 'outsider' to 'insider' in the implementation of change, I realize that I do not function alone, but act within a whole dynamic. Ideas are conceived by individuals or groups, within and without the college, filtered down from above or arising freshly from the grass roots: ideas derived from reading, living, talking, visiting and thinking. It is the altered context or implementation of these ideas that is designated 'change'.

Real change occurs when enough of us accept that the 'change' is the obvious next step. But then it is not change – it *is* merely the next step. I believe that my role is to facilitate that step. I do this by serving as a two-way communication between senior management and the rest of the college community: communicating by talking to others, setting small schemes in motion, reporting and retelling, reinforcing and encouraging; familiarizing people with new ideas and reducing the threat of the unknown thus assisting our community to move forward along that path laid down over 155 years ago.

My final observation about change focuses on the legitimization provided by senior management. Without support from this team, initiation and maintenance of change would be difficult. The confidence that they instil in me as an individual, by listening to my ideas, by trusting me to deliver and by allowing space for failure and redemption, is incalculable. I believe that, just as I hope to continue being treated in this positive way, so too will I treat others who are beginning to venture into the management of change. I believe that it is in this way that our characteristic sense of community will continue to work to the advantage and progress of us all at the college.

REFERENCE

Bradbury, JL (1975) *Chester College and the Training of Teachers 1839–1975*, Seabourne Collection: The Governors of Chester College.

Chapter 11

Student Unions and Universities in Partnership – The Future of Higher Education?

Lee Whitehead

THE SHOCK

It was April 1993. I had just bought myself a new chair to celebrate the fact that I had been re-elected as president of the University of Glamorgan union for a second term of office. It was in this high-backed, soft, black executive chair (with arms) that I reclined as I contemplated the next year at the University of Glamorgan.

The university had just metamorphosed from the Polytechnic of Wales, which itself had just months beforehand quietly snipped itself free from the apron-strings of Mid-Glamorgan Council to become a brand, spanking new higher education corporation. The university had just appointed its first vice-chancellor who took up office in April. The university had just recovered from taking in more students than it could accommodate at the start of term, hence the near catastrophe that was the 'Barry Island Holiday Camp' incident which saw students billeted in decaying surroundings 25 miles from campus during their first weeks at the university. Then, just to add the icing to the cake, the Higher Education Funding Council for Wales (HEFC(W)) had decided that the university had to submit a five-year strategic plan by the start of July.

I curled up in my new chair and contemplated the union's problems. We were in the middle of planning a major refurbishment programme, writing our own strategic plan for commercial services and had just undertaken the most fundamental re-appraisal of our democratic structures that had resulted in an entirely new constitution (University of Glamorgan, 1992). The new constitution had been written from scratch giving students greater direct input into union policy through referenda, while improving the day-to-day decision making of the union by increasing the number of officers in the sabbatical team and setting up a union council. Then, finally, the Secretary of State for Education at the time was trying to destroy the student movement with legislation which would have split the functions of student unions into various public-funded and non-public-funded areas of work. This would have meant the destruction of student unions and the National Union of Students as representative organizations campaigning on behalf of students on education matters. The proposed legislation would also have seen the end of bars, shops, launderettes, student newspapers and a whole plethora of other commercial and non-commercial services currently controlled by students for the use of students.

The union was busy enough with its own problems as I sat and contemplated the university and its impending strategy project. A plan started to form in my head: the way for the union to deal with the university and its problems. The way to input into strategic planning. The way to make the union indispensable to the university.

The answer to the question of strategic planning from a union point of view was a wide-ranging and fundamental programme of 'masterly inactivity' followed by a perfect performance of a Pontius Pilate-type hand manoeuvre if things went wrong. This was the accepted student union way: stay outside and criticize, appear Left and confrontational, be populist and produce a shopping list of demands, have them rejected and then get re-elected. The decision was made. I was content. The union was safe from pillory amongst its sister institutions and its own students. We would object to the plan for attempting to fit more students into already constricted space, pass a general meeting policy of condemnation and then concentrate on our own problems.

My phone rang, the white one, the internal university one, somebody from the University wanted to speak to me. Not a problem, that happened all the time. 'Hello, Lee Whitehead speaking, can I help you' – my best customer-care voice. 'Can you hold please?' I recognized the voice immediately, it was the vice-chancellor's secretary; 'The vice-chancellor would like a word.' She put me on hold and my mind started to race. Was there trouble in the bar last night? Have the police been on the phone? Was the government about to abolish student unions and my new VC was ringing up to say good riddance? Had they finished the strategic plan already and he was ringing up to warn me about the doubling in student numbers and what my response should be if I knew what my block-grant was good for? No! it was much worse than all the thoughts that had flashed through my fevered brain: 'Hello Lee, Adrian here. We need to get together and have a chat about how the union is going to input into the strategic planning. I want the union to be at the centre of providing real student input into the plan'.

THE IMMEDIATE REACTION

I stammered an agreement, arranged a date, put the phone on the hook then placed my head in my hands and sobbed gently. All my plans destroyed; the university actually wanted our input, we were to be inculcated into the decisions of the university. Oh! the shame of it; what about the rent-strikes? The occupations? The demonstrations? The revolution? How was I to find the time? I could see the faces of the students and some of my sadder peers in the student movement now: 'Sell-out... scab... teacher's pet... management lackey'. I went home determined to discuss with my house-mate, who also happened to be the union deputy president, education and welfare, the best way to drag the union out of this hole in which it found itself.

We sat and argued and cogitated and digested long into the early hours of the morning. It was a trap to implicate us in the strategic process, about that I had no doubt. It would make our response that much harder; it was a ploy I had used before with opposition within the union. The obvious choice was to follow the normal form for these occasions and play the 'shopping list' card, then we could say we had made an effort to contribute but had been thwarted by management. That was the easy way, that was the traditional student union way. It was not the way we decided to go.

The way we approached the problem brought into question the whole perceived ethos and history of student unions. Was confrontation and distancing yourself from the real decision-making structures the best way to represent the students who elected you? I had long thought not and the executive we had built thought not. This was an opportunity as well as a trap. We decided that the way to deal with this conundrum was to grab the opportunity and dextrously avoid the trap being laid in the process by being radical.

We decided at 4 o'clock in the morning, in our by now Coke-can-strewn living room, that we were going to implement a series of meetings with students, sabbatical officers and union staff that would enable the union to write its own version of a strategic plan for the university. The document was going to break the long-held views and tactics of the student union movement. We were going to be positive, radical and detailed and we were going to stand behind everything we wrote.

THE STRATEGY

As well as the formal implementation of the strategic plan concept groups, which would be responsible for drawing on the experience of people from all across the university in order to flesh out a plan, the new vice-chancellor had decided that the university required a root-and-branch review of itself, how it worked (or didn't work) and what staff and students thought of the institution. To this end the university had employed the services of an external consulting group experienced in working with, and helping to manage, change in the public sector. We decided that the union should immerse itself completely in the work of the external consultancy team and attempt to use the lessons we learnt from this process to good effect when it came to writing our strategic submission.

The executive committee of the union met the next day and decided that the idea of the 'University of Glamorgan Union Strategic Plan Submission' was one that they supported. We recognized that we were doing something different. We were taking a step into largely uncharted waters as regards university/union relations. We were going to talk about partnership not conflict. We were not going to demand unrealistic staff:student ratios and a huge new library as catch-all problem solvers. We were going to address the market in higher education and recognize the limitations and opportunities that it placed on the university. We were not going to say nothing could be done unless the government pumped billions of pounds into the system and leave our response at that. We were going to be realistic and create a plan from the students' point of view which would fit into the present framework of higher education in Wales. We were going to attempt to win real victories, not just high-principled, moral arguments.

The process

The external consultancy team had developed a way of working within the university which I found helpful and which we utilized when we started to involve students in our submission. The concept of 'slice groups' was one which we were to use extensively during the following few weeks. A slice group consists of a small representative sample of a population, in this case students, being brought together to discuss and analyse a particular subject. The groups are not just about getting opinions from people; they are about discussion and feedback in a structured environment within the group. When the consultants decided that they wanted to find out student views and feelings about the university they asked the union to produce a cross-section of students and union officers. We decided that we would use the same group of students for the initial stages of our strategic submission.

The beginning

The students were from a wide range of courses, ages, methods of study and both sexes. There were 12 students and three sabbatical officers of the union, all of whom had been involved to some extent in working with the external consultancy team and therefore were broadly comfortable with the process and reasonably knowledgeable about the university and its structures. We felt that a level of understanding was needed to make the best possible use of the initial blank-page meeting. This session started with an explanation of what was desired and then developed into a brainstorm with a note-taker and flipchart.

The students were presented with the information that *we needed to produce a university strategic plan for submission to the university to a high enough standard that the university could submit it to the HEFC(W) untouched.*

In this first meeting I acted as coordinator and furnisher of answers should specific questions require answering with regards to the university, union policy, government policy, etc, but largely stayed out of the policy discussion. The object of this meeting was to establish a theme for the document and an idea of the specific items which required attention and further discussion, as well as the basic principles that would drive the whole document.

By the end of the three-hour-long meeting we had a whole pad of flipchart paper of feedback, ideas, principles and the outline of a mission statement. It was then my job to go and write an initial draft of the document within the framework provided by the HEFC(W) on the theme that had been decided by that initial meeting: *the quality of the whole student experience.*

There then followed a week and a half of slaving over a hot word-processor to produce an initial draft that included:

- a revised mission statement;
- a departmental plan for the student union;
- an academic development plan;
- a resource and implementation strategy

as well as sections regarding character, opportunities and external factors. The initial draft of the plan stretched to 14 pages and included over 70 separate recommendations and observations running to 5,000 words. It was, we felt at the time, one of the most radical development plans ever to see the light of day from a student union.

The initial document included references to a 'constructive entry into the debate on tri-semesterization' and its possible effects on accelerated degrees and staff deployment; an abandonment of overseas franchise courses; a 'University of the Valleys' outreach programme of community education; a commitment to fully funding the enterprise unit beyond Employment Department funding; an extension of the Credit Accumulation and Transfer Scheme to include student union and community work through specific module development; customer care training for all university front-line staff; new student feedback procedures; a programme of teaching qualifications for all lecturers; the development of learner agreements and student charters; decision-making skills training for all staff that attend committees; the abolition of the academic departmental structure to facilitate a modular course structure; a proposal for anonymous marking; and a commitment to student union funding regardless of government intervention.

The plan talked about competition with the University of Wales (the federal university which includes all the other university colleges in Wales), commercial consultancy by university staff, responsibilities, as well as rights, of the student and an understanding of the financial position of the university without attempting to score political points by apportioning blame. The plan was a completely different animal from historical, overtly political student union attempts to influence university thinking and policy. As the author, and the senior elected student representative, I now faced the acid test of how 'real' students would react to the document.

The progress

We now presented the report to two slice groups. The first consisted of the same people who had set the original theme, but the second was a new group of students who had not been part of the process up until this stage. The groups met separately and went through the document word for word. There were debates about whether we should be constructive, positive or destructive about tri-semesterization (result: constructive with provisos regarding funding). There were debates about mentioning the educational market or the competition by name (result: University of Wales got a mention). There were debates about whether students were customer, consumer, product or owner of education (result: consumer with active policy-making powers).

There was, however, no debate about the strategy of full participation and support for the strategic planning process that the union was following because no debate was needed. It was accepted that we were doing the right thing. We had gone into this exercise thinking we were being brave and radical but the students thought we were just being sensible and representative, which was after all what they elected us for and pay us to do.

THE DOCUMENT AND THE UNIVERSITY

On the basis of these meetings and further consultation with students through a widely available summary of the document, we finished the production of the plan and felt that we had moved into a new area of student representation at the University of Glamorgan. The document was completed by the end of May and was published with a print run of 100 to the university staff, management, governors and local student unions (University of Glamorgan Union, 1993a).

The report was broadly greeted as a constructive and welcome input into the strategic planning debate. The university found much more to disagree with in the document than our students had. The document had ruffled the feathers of many vested interests: departments did not want to be abolished; lecturers did not want to be trained to teach; porters thought their approach to customer care was fine; learner agreements were far too complicated and could result in litigation; and overseas franchises raised money. The plan as a whole was something we were proud of. It followed a theme of quality of the student experience from the introduction and mission statement through to the conclusion, which states:

> *We feel that this document provides a sound, but radical base for the University to compete in the Higher Education market, and in five years time to have carved out the proverbial niche based on true innovation and the student life experience.*

Despite reservations on some of the specific details from individual areas of the university, the overall theme and strategy of the union received widespread support amongst university staff, management and governors. The mission statement was discussed by the academic board with a strong lobby of support forming for the statement simply to replace the university's present statement. The chair of governors proposed separate funding for the safety audit of campus put forward in the plan. The head of higher education development at the consultancy organization employed by the university remarked that it was one of the best development plans she had ever seen in higher education. The plan had a fundamental effect on the eventual university plan and many of the individual recommendations have since seen the light of day through various university initiatives.

THE FOLLOW-UP

The project represented the beginning of a new working relationship between the university and the student union. The days of conflict and confrontation, that had once seen the union refuse to play a role in the Enterprise in Higher Education Initiative because it was the 'beginning of the privatization of education' were gone, to be replaced by an era of partnership and trust.

Over the next few months the student union played a progressively more active role in the management and policy-making of the university. I, as president, was included in a sub-committee of governors – the first time a student union officer had been included at such a level – charged with creating a new management structure for the university in consultation with outside management consultants. The union was central to the conception and implementation of a university-wide 'First experience project' designed to coordinate a package of initiatives to ensure the best possible experience for new students at the university. Such faith was placed in the union that I was actually responsible for running a courier system during the first few weeks of term that involved direction of university staff and a budget approaching £10,000. As president of the union I was also sent as the sole university representative to many academic conferences, with the remit to report back to the academic board and the quality and standards committee. I presently sit on the working group preparing the university for the visit of the Academic Audit Unit in December. The president has equal space in the official university prospectus as the vice-chancellor to welcome new students. The effect of our new relationship has seen real, concrete results for the union and the students of the university.

Since the excellent reception of the paper on strategic planning, and as a continuation of our 'special relationship', the union has developed an in-house system and style for presenting and following-up proposals to the university. The author may be an individual member of the executive but the work must go through the president, executive and the newly formed union council before being presented to the university. This system has seen the union produce policy and strategy papers such as:

- Student Charters – A Proposal
- The Case for Anonymous Marking
- A Harassment Policy
- An Equal Opportunities Statement
- The Courier Proposals
- Capital Building Expenditure – The Students' Voice
- A Student Union Reform Briefing Pack
- Measuring Student Satisfaction – A Report
- An Accommodation Strategy for the University.

We believe that this sort of professional, well-presented information has seen a marked increase in the esteem in which the union is held by the management and staff of the university and therefore the ability of the union to influence the university has increased by equal measure.

The relationship between the union and the university has developed into one built on trust and a mutual respect for competence. We do not always agree; we still have arguments and disagreements but these disagreements are fought out between people who can sit and talk and then deliver on promises made. The idea that the way to deal with problems in the halls of residences is by a rent-strike is no longer part of the culture of the university. The days of occupying the university administration office over government policy are now behind us.

It is the sort of relationship between university and union which is productive and led to the union receiving unconditional support from the university in the recent campaign against the Department for Education and their plans to introduce curbs on student unions. It is a relationship that will be built on in the future.

THE FUTURE

One year later the students of the University of Glamorgan showed their support for a strategy of realistic negotiation and partnership between university and union by electing a new sabbatical team that supported and played a part in the new partnership. The students rejected strategies put forward by rival candidates that played the 'present union is a disgraceful management lackey' card. They recognized that the way the union was presently working was gaining real benefits for them, including increased safety measures on campus, student input into the design of a new £7.5m block of student residences, increased space and services in their own union through loans and grants from the university and better negotiated deals with the refectory for on-campus resident students.

The ethos of partnership and cooperation is now so embedded in the new university structures and personnel that headed notepaper is presently being produced with the logos of the union and university side by side, with the legend '...Working together to serve you.' I believe that this sort of relationship, unheard of in the recent history of the great university and union battles of the 1980s, is the way forward.

CONCLUSION

The further and higher education system in Britain is undergoing radical stop/go government-led growth and reform. The composition of our student body is markedly different from that of even five years ago, with the increase in mature students being the most noticeable change. The change in university structures, with the abolition of the binary divide and imposition of corporate status; the invention of 'franchise' courses and the increase in part-time provision – these particular examples are just some of the changes that have affected the system while seeing it progressively pushed further and further into a cash-starved corner. The role of the student representative voice has not steeped itself in glory during this time.

There have been examples of good conduct. The student charter initiatives at Liverpool John Moores University and Oxford Brookes University have been supported and actively encouraged by the student unions. The union strategic planning project at the University of Warwick has seen real student input into an excellent idea for developing and restructuring the union in the light of the new priorities and ideals the union has. The cooperation between unions and universities in Leeds to provide student housing by setting up an accommodation management, information and inspection service has derived benefits for individual students on a large-scale basis. However, these examples are unfortunately the exception rather than the rule. There have been far too many easy answers offered by student union officers; the 'organize, occupy and generally misbehave' school of unions are still leading students down the blind alleys of opposition to government by blaming university administrations. At the other end of the scale are the union officers more interested in bar profits and their own self-importance while playing at politics by opposing the ultra- (and sometimes not so ultra-)Left as a substitute for positive student-centred work and representation. Neither of these ways represents a viable future for student unionism.

It is the job of a student union to provide services, both commercial and non-commercial, to their students while continuing the representation and campaigning which should be at the heart of the student movement. Campaigning is important, but the tactics are more important. It is time for unions and their officers to realize that partnership and negotiation will win them more battles for their students than outright confrontation. It is time for union officers to lead where students will follow, because they will find that most students were there beforehand waiting for their union to catch up.

It is time for student unions to realize that the education system will continue to change with or without their cooperation. Those unions which involve themselves in the management of change will ensure that student welfare is at the centre of change, whereas those that stand back and oppose from without will find they have no influence. These unions will do a disservice not only to their own students but also to any changes that will not have the benefit of student input, thereby intrinsically devaluing the changes and setting-up possible problems in the future, for students, when the changes are implemented.

At a time of change in higher education, student unions should be winning victories, not just high-principled, moral arguments. The time has come for partnership and responsibility and I am glad that the threat of legislation and the new breed of union officers are hastening the process.

NOTE

The Office for Public Management is an independent management consultancy organization specializing in cultural change strategies and organization development strategies in the public sector under the banner, 'Managing for social change'. The work they did for the University of Glamorgan (and union) was vital in the managing of change at the institution in the last two years.

REFERENCES

University of Glamorgan (1992), *Union Constitution.*

University of Glamorgan Union (1993a), *Submission to the University of Glamorgan Strategic Plan 1993–1998.*

University of Glamorgan (1993b), *Strategic Plan 1993–1998.*

Appendix

Growth and Diversity: A New Era in Colleges and Universities*

Rhodri Phillips

Views expressed in this chapter are personal and do not necessarily reflect the views of CVCP.

INTRODUCTION

Higher education in Britain has rarely been in a steady state. It has continuously been pushed by two conflicting pressures: to maximize its contribution to society and the economy, and to control public expenditure. Nevertheless the changes that have taken place since the mid-1980s have been the most momentous since the period following the publication of the Robbins Report in 1963, and have changed the face of higher education.

The purpose of this chapter is to provide a broad context of the changes that have and are likely to take place in higher education. It examines the interrelationship of three factors: quantity, quality and funding. In teaching, for example, there has been concern that the growth in student numbers but a decline in funding per student has lowered quality. This chapter concentrates on teaching within a simple model, shown in Figure A.1, and on universities and colleges of HE.

The distinction between HE and FE is a legal and administrative convenience, based on the educational standard of the course, but in reality the two are closely intertwined. Many colleges of further education run higher education courses and vice versa. The Further and Higher Education Act 1992 did not only complete the reorganization of higher education; it also gave colleges of further education their independence from local government and set them on the path followed by polytechnics and colleges of higher education four years earlier after the 1988 Act. Although their roles may differ to some extent, the issues they face are very similar.

* This Appendix is also contained in the companion volume, *Introducing Change 'From the Top' of Universities and Colleges,* edited by Susan Weil.

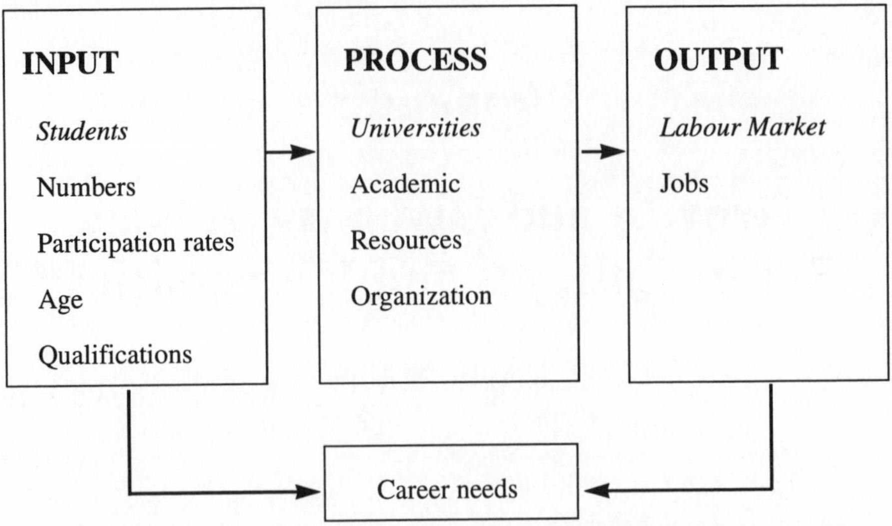

Figure A.1

GOVERNMENT POLICY FRAMEWORK

The Conservative government that came to power in July 1979 saw itself as engaged in a mission of reform and renewal but in its early years its policy changes in education concentrated largely on schools. This changed in 1987 with the publication of the White Paper *Higher Education: Meeting the Challenge* (DES, 1987) which proposed major changes to the organization of higher education:

- a growth in participation rates among young and mature students in higher education and some growth in FTE student numbers;
- the replacement of the University Grants Committee by the Universities Funding Council (UFC) to fund all British universities;
- the creation of a Polytechnics and Colleges Funding Council (PCFC) to fund polytechnics, colleges of higher education, voluntary and other grant-aided colleges in England (those in Scotland and Wales continued to be funded by local authorities).

These changes were enacted in the Education Reform Act 1988 and the UFC and the PCFC took on their new responsibilities on 1 April 1989.

The increase in full-time student numbers proposed in the 1987 White Paper was relatively modest. A radical policy was introduced in 1989/90 when tuition fees paid by local education authorities were sharply increased as an inducement to institutions to expand faster, encouraging a growth in student numbers and reducing the cost per student, while maintaining quality. The target was one in three young people in higher education by the year 2000.

The 1987 White Paper set out the government's agenda which runs as a continuous thread through subsequent years:

- wider access to higher education for young people with qualifications other than A levels, and for mature people;
- continuing part-time higher education for those in employment who wished to improve their professional knowledge and skills;
- improvements in the design and content of courses and in quality of teaching;
- greater emphasis on quality in research;
- increased efficiency of institutions, measured by performance indicators.

The 1991 White Paper, *Higher Education: A New Framework* (DES, 1991) made more radical proposals to reorganize higher education and to continue the drive to increase efficiency and quality:

- separate Higher Education Funding Councils (HEFCs) in England, Wales and Scotland funding all higher education institutions in those countries;
- the upgrading of polytechnics to university status and the extension to them of degree-awarding status with the consequent winding up of the Council for National Academic Awards (CNAA);
- the introduction of new measures on quality assurance, including a quality assessment role for the HEFCs and a quality audit unit developed by institutions.

These changes were included in the Further and Higher Education Act 1992.

By 1994, the government saw itself as having 'solved' the issue of higher education. The sector had been reorganized, numbers of students had grown and issues of quality were being addressed. As the government saw it, the onus was now on the universities and colleges themselves – cajoled by the HEFCs – to make a mass higher education system work efficiently and effectively. A policy of 'consolidation' was introduced tentatively in 1993/4, but it is the government's intention that it will be rigidly enforced in 1994/5 and subsequent years as part of the containment of public expenditure.

GROWTH IN TEACHING

It is worth examining the extent and pattern of growth in student numbers since the late 1980s as a mass higher education system has been created. The rate of growth in home student numbers exceeded the forecasts of both the 1987 and the 1991 White Papers, and targets set for the end of the decade had already been achieved by 1993/4.

The total number of students rose by over 50 per cent but there were wide variations between levels and modes (full- and part-time). Postgraduate numbers, particularly on part-time and distance learning courses, grew particularly fast. At undergraduate level, the big increase was in numbers on full-time courses (see Table A.1).

The increase in numbers on undergraduate courses was achieved by increased participation in higher education by all age groups, but particularly by mature students aged 21 and over when they entered courses. The age participation index of

18–19-year-olds (ie, the proportion entering higher education) rose from 14.6 per cent in 1987/8 to 31 per cent in 1993/4 (close to the target that was planned to be achieved by the end of the decade). But numbers of older entrants grew faster, and in 1993/4 formed over half the undergraduate students at some new universities in urban areas (see unpublished statistics).

Table A.1 Growth in home student numbers (in thousands)

	1988/9	1993/4	Growth %
Undergraduate			
Full-time	517	866	68
Part-time	233	276	18
Open University	82	97	18
Total	832	1239	49
Postgraduate			
Full-time	47	76	62
Part-time	59	111	88
Open University	3	11	267
Total	109	198	82
TOTAL	941	1437	53

Source: DfE unpublished statistics

Growth in undergraduate numbers was not evenly spread among subjects. Despite the popular view that growth has been largely in the humanities and social sciences, numbers in science subjects as a whole grew at the same rate – 31 per cent – as non-science subjects. But this masked wide variations. Among the large academic areas, growth was particularly high on undergraduate education courses but below average on physical sciences and engineering.

The proportion of 18–19-year-olds in England and Wales achieving two A level passes – the basic entry requirement to degree courses – rose slowly but steadily in the late 1980s and early 1990s to 21.8 per cent in 1991/2 but this was well below the current rate of entry to higher education in 1993/4. Many enter full-time and sandwich first degree courses in England without A levels but – surprisingly, in the perception of most staff within universities – the average score of those entrants with A levels has risen (DfE, 1994).

The evidence on wastage rates on first degree courses is inconclusive. In England, they have fluctuated between 14 and 17 per cent from year to year, but there was no evidence by 1991/2 of an upward trend, although more recent figures may be different when they are published. The academic quality of entrants does not appear to have declined, which would have contributed to the stability in wastage rates. Indeed the evidence of degree standards is that the proportion of students on full-time and sandwich courses achieving good degrees (defined as first and upper second degrees) rose (DfE, 1994).

Looking to the future, the government's policy on consolidation means that there will be only small growth in full-time student numbers on higher education courses funded by the HEFCs. Those institutions which wish to continue to expand their teaching provision will have to look for growth in other areas:

- *full-time:* nursing and other courses funded by health authorities (which accounts for why many universities are seeking to take over nursing colleges), self-funded professional courses, overseas students;
- *part-time:* undergraduate and particularly postgraduate courses provided they are run in twilight hours or at weekends (the evidence is that day-release is disappearing in the face of employers' reluctance to release employees during working hours).

Part-time postgraduate, or rather post-experience, education may provide one of the most important expanding markets over the rest of the decade. The notion that individuals take responsibility for the education and training linked to their career development, as set out in the CBI's careership proposals (CBI, 1993), appears to be gaining ground. Those who have already taken an undergraduate course are increasingly prepared to study further on Masters, advanced diploma or non-assessed courses. Lifelong learning will require employers to become learning organizations and universities to provide more individually-oriented teaching and learning approaches (Lloyd, 1992).

The projections of the Department for Education (DfE) and the Committee of Vice-chancellors and Principals (CVCP) of undergraduate and postgraduate numbers to the year 2000 envisage some continued growth, particularly after the end of the current public expenditure planning period in 1996/7. DfE/CVCP projections for full-time undergraduate numbers are based on the planning assumption that the age participation index among 18–19-year-olds will gradually rise to 33 per cent by the end of the decade. This would give some 220,000 entrants aged 18–19 with a further 100,000 mature entrants aged over 21. However the proportion of 18–19-year-olds entering higher education could be much greater if numbers of young entrants expand at the expense of older entrants within the overall planning total. Whether such a shift in the age of entrants would take place would depend to a large extent on the central policy of each university and the decisions of admissions tutors.

It is expected that the expansion in 16–19 education and the introduction of General National Vocational Qualifications (GNVQs) will increase the number of 18–19-year-olds with suitable qualifications for entry to higher education. The national training and education targets envisage 50 per cent of the age group achieving GNVQ level 3 by the year 2000 (DES/ED, 1991). The development of GNVQs has been criticized (Smithers, 1993), for such things as the lack of syllabuses, time limits, written examinations and external tests, and changes are likely. The lack of scores on GNVQs for admissions tutors might limit GNVQ students to the local university with which their college has links (in contrast to A level students with a 'portable' qualification leading to entry at any university).

TEACHING FUNDING

The funding regimes under which universities and colleges have operated have changed twice – from 'stop' to 'go' and then back to 'stop' – in the last five years to reflect changes in government policy on student numbers. However, it is fair to say that the change from 'stop' to 'go' has been easier to implement than the reverse, because institutions have entered long-term commitments in the growth period (principally on staffing and property) which must continue to be financed.

When the UFC and PCFC were set up, new funding arrangements were introduced with two objectives: to increase the numbers of publicly-funded students and to reduce the public funding per full- and part-time student while maintaining quality. This was to be achieved in three ways:

- the grant and fee per student rose by the Treasury's internal inflation index (called the GDP deflator), which was always less than the retail price index increase each year;
- efficiency gains were required each year;
- the UFC and PCFC introduced bidding systems to enable institutions to bid for additional funds placed at the margin below the average grant per student.

The first two have been central to all government expenditure programmes over the past decade and are not unique to higher education; the third operated differently within the UFC and PCFC sectors. The UFC published a guide price at which all universities bid so that funded numbers and grant per student remained largely unchanged. In contrast, the PCFC required polytechnics and colleges to bid a small part of numbers funded in the previous year. The polytechnics and colleges responded with aggressive bidding down of the marginal grant per student.

While the UFC and PCFC were devising their new funding methodologies, the government announced a very large shift of funding from grant to fees and non-cash-limited funding for fees. This provided a big financial incentive for institutions to take on additional students at the margin. The recruitment of fees-only students had a much greater effect in reducing the total funding per student than the Funding Councils' competitive bidding mechanisms. Over 30 per cent of the students at some institutions were recruited on a fees-only basis.

Universities on the one hand and some polytechnics and colleges on the other, adopted different strategies. Universities were concerned at the effect of declining funding per student on the quality of teaching and at the effect of increased student numbers on research quality. They were therefore cautious in their growth plans. Polytechnics and large general colleges (small specialist colleges were different) took the opposite view. They were committed to widening access to higher education and saw growth as desirable in itself. They also wished to increase their market share and maximize their teaching income (their only major source of income at that time) before the government ended the period of growth. With marginal revenue being greater than marginal cost, growth yielded larger surpluses which could be ploughed back into the institution. The result was a growth of 68 per cent in the amount of public money in real terms devoted to higher education between 1988/9 and 1994/5; but funding per student has declined and will continue to do so (DfE, 1994).

The creation of the three new HEFCs in 1992 coincided with the government's decision to end the period of growth in student numbers because its targets had been met. There have been three changes in the funding mechanism to ensure that institutions maintain their present numbers of students but do not increase them:

- In 1993/4 the HEFC in England incorporated fees-only students into funded numbers at each institution (with a consequent fall in the grant per student depending on the number of fees-only students in that institution). This grant per student was called an Average Unit of Council Funding (AUCF) and differed among 11 academic subject categories. The result was that institutions could not reduce their intake without losing HEFCE grant.
- The classroom-based course fee rate was reduced marginally in 1993/4, with little effect on recruitment. It will be reduced by 45 per cent in each of the three fee rates in 1994/5. Existing students will be protected by an increase in HEFC grant but any financial incentive to recruit fees-only students will be removed.
- To reinforce the message of the fees reduction, the HEFCs will penalize any recruitment above 1993/4 levels in 1994/5.

The abrupt change from growth to consolidation caused many problems for those institutions which planned to grow fast in the mid-1990s, principally in the former PCFC sector. The strategic plans of polytechnics and colleges prepared in 1992 (PCFC, 1992b) envisaged a substantial growth in home student numbers between 1991/2 and 1995/6. Income was planned to grow by 43 per cent during this period, and tuition fee income (including that from overseas students) by 75 per cent. Polytechnics and colleges planned to invest heavily in premises and staff and some had begun to do so on the basis that growth would continue. For example, large increases in teaching accommodation were planned in this period: 20 per cent across the sector and 137 per cent in larger colleges; an increase of 15 per cent in full-time academic staff was also planned. Those institutions which had to service long-term commitments without the growth for which these had been entered into found that they had to make radical readjustments in their financial forecasts.

As university and college funding has changed under public expenditure constraints, so has the funding of students themselves on full-time undergraduate courses. Student loans were introduced in 1990/91 and from 1994/5 maintenance awards will be reduced by 10 per cent a year for three years and the equivalent amount of money added to the maximum student loan. By 1996/7, maintenance awards and loans will be approximately equal. This will mean a sharp increase in student indebtedness.

Looking to the future, there is common ground between the government and the CVCP that the effect of public expenditure constraints on the quality of higher education will require an increasing financial contribution from full-time students in future. A report commissioned by CVCP from London Economics (CVCP, 1993) set out various options for a student contribution to tuition fees. There is no indication that the government will require a contribution by full-time students to tuition costs in the next few years; instead it is pursuing the switch from maintenance awards to loans described above.

TEACHING EFFICIENCY

An important item on the government's agenda is an increase in 'efficiency'. The latest government expenditure plans (DfE, 1994) acknowledge that institutions have:

> *achieved significant reductions in unit costs in recent years as student numbers have grown. These reductions have been accompanied by maintained or increased quality, and thus represent productivity gains...The scale of the gains has exceeded those planned by the Government as a result of institutions' decisions to recruit at or above the level of the Government's plans.*

Improvements in efficiency are to be measured by performance indicators. The CVCP has for several years produced an annual volume of university management statistics which have set out detailed figures for every university. A PCFC committee of enquiry produced a report (PCFC, 1990) with recommendations for indicators for the sector as a whole and for individual institutions. This subsequently resurfaced in a PCFC report on macro performance indicators (PCFC, 1992a). Performance indicators are now being revisited by a joint working group of the HEFCs and CVCP and a report will emerge in 1994 with a wealth of indicators on teaching quality, research, finance, estates and much else. The intention is that indicators for all institutions should be published to increase accountability.

Performance indicators have in the past been intended to assist the Funding Councils and institutions themselves. Despite the mass of data collected, it is difficult to point to many decisions taken on the basis of performance indicators. It is unclear whether widening the audience to include the public will change this.

Another strand to efficiency, particularly in premises use, is the proposal to introduce a third semester in the summer vacation in institutions which have reordered this academic year. A report published in 1993 (HEFCE, 1993) made proposals which would bring the start of the autumn semester to the beginning of September. This idea was born out of the period of growth and was intended to enable institutions to take on more students without additional investment in premises. Since growth has now been curtailed, the proposals seem less relevant.

TEACHING QUALITY

The 1987 White Paper defined quality in terms of:

- academic standards as reflected by the design and content of courses, their fitness for purpose, what they require of students and how they meet the needs of employers;
- the quality of teaching;
- the achievements of students, both while in higher education and in subsequent employment;
- the quality of research.

The then universities were entirely and solely responsible for the quality of teaching in their own institutions. The Committee of Vice-chancellors and Principals published in 1986 a code of practice on academic standards and monitored its observance. CVCP further decided in 1989 to set up an Academic Audit Unit to review institutions' systems for quality. The Unit began work in 1990, aiming to visit and report on every UFC institution within three years. The 1987 White Paper (DES, 1987) nevertheless registered the government's concern that 'universities, individually and collectively, should do more to reassure the public about the ways in which they control standards'.

In contrast, academic standards in polytechnics and colleges were controlled and monitored at three levels:

- the then CNAA approved the academic content of degree courses to ensure that standards were comparable with those in universities. In practice, all polytechnics were accredited to approve individual courses at undergraduate level (and some at postgraduate level);
- the Business and Technician Education Council (BTEC) approved courses below degree level, principally Higher National Diploma and Certificate courses;
- Her Majesty's Inspectorate (HMI) inspected and reported on all courses.

The PCFC took steps both to define and promote quality and to reward good quality through its funding mechanism. A report was prepared by a Committee on Teaching Quality chaired by Baroness Warnock which, unfortunately, became lost in philosophical discussions and did not take the debate much further. In contrast, HMI produced a five-point scale for assessing quality which was used to reward academic programmes whose quality was judged to be excellent and to withdraw funding from those judged to be unacceptable (a threat never carried out).

The 1991 White Paper (DES, 1991) took a much firmer grip on the quality issue. It stressed the related requirements for accountability and information:

> *There is a need for proper accountability for the substantial public funds invested in higher education. As part of this, students and employers need improved information about quality if the full benefit of increased competition is to be obtained.*

It distinguished between

- *quality control:* mechanisms within institutions for maintaining and enhancing the quality of their provision;
- *quality audit:* external scrutiny aimed at providing guarantees that institutions have suitable quality control mechanisms in place;
- *quality assessment:* external review of, and judgements about, the quality of teaching and learning in institutions.

The recommendations on both quality assessment and quality audit were later implemented. Quality assessment was introduced in the Further and Higher Education Act 1992 which requires the HEFCs to 'secure that provision is made for assessing the quality of education in those institutions for whose activities they provide, or are considering providing, financial support'. Each HEFC has set up different but similar arrangements to assess quality in each academic area. They involve a varying mixture of self-assessment and in some cases an institutional visit by a team of assessors drawn from senior staff at other universities. The HEFCs issue a rating on a three-point scale: excellent, satisfactory and unsatisfactory (although the Scottish HEFC has decided to use a four-point scale in future).

There has been some criticism of the way that assessments have been carried out in England (less so in Scotland and Wales). It has been said that the assessment teams have given greater weight to research background and traditional teaching methods such as lectures, and have rated less highly innovative teaching methods to the students from non-traditional backgrounds who have made up much of the growth in higher education. It is certainly true that the older universities in England have done far better in the assessment exercise than the new universities, which have prided themselves on their teaching quality.

The HEFC for England published an independent report into the assessment process (HEFCE, 1994b). Its most important recommendations were that visits should be extended to cover all departments and academic programmes and that the judgemental component should be modified to indicate whether the department is operating at a threshold level of sound provision. This latter recommendation would replace the three-point scale. The initial response of the HEFC in England to this recommendation was hostile.

The universities and colleges set up the Higher Education Quality Council (HEQC) to deal with quality audit, replacing the former CVCP academic audit unit. All institutions are required to be subject to the HEQC under the terms of the financial memorandum with their Funding Council. The HEQC appoints teams of senior academics at universities to examine the mechanisms and structures in place in each university and college to ensure quality. The overall impression to emerge has been that institutions that came within the ambit of the former CNAA have had to have appropriate processes in place, but that the formalization of these processes has been more recent in some of the older universities.

A potentially more important longer-term issue is the views of students on the quality of their higher education as they contribute to an increasing proportion of its cost. The government published a Higher Education Charter in 1993 (DfE, 1993) which set out in general terms certain minimum standards that students should be able to expect. Several studies have been carried out to establish the views of students (Roberts *et al.,* 1992; SBU, 1993; UCE, 1993). They found a broad range of dissatisfactions, from lecturing methods to buildings and facilities, which increased as student numbers grew. The UCE report noted that:

> *Students are somewhat bored with the traditional 'chalk and talk' approach and would welcome a variety of teaching methods and the new pattern of learning activities that this would inculcate.*

A large part of the growth in full-time undergraduate numbers has taken place on courses or parts of courses (typically foundation years) franchised from universities to colleges of further education. These links have been important in widening access. In 1993 some 25,000 to 30,000 students were estimated to be on such courses. An

HEQC report (HEQC, 1993) found that the quality of student experience in the classroom was comparable to that of equivalent courses in higher education institutions although the supporting facilities were not always up to the same standard. The future of many of these courses is uncertain as the funding arrangements have changed.

A key measure of output quality is graduate employment. The labour market has had to adapt over recent years both to fewer 18-year-olds seeking employment as higher education expanded, and to more graduates seeking jobs. The process of adaptation is far from complete in 1994.

The number of students graduating from courses rose by 22 per cent between 1987/8 and 1991/2, from 99,000 to 121,000. This growth coincided with the beginning of the recession, which makes it more difficult to identify a long-term trend. Nevertheless, the latest available figures (DfE, 1994) show that less than half of first degree graduates in summer 1992 in England obtained jobs in the UK and the proportion pursuing further courses or remaining unemployed has risen sharply. The labour market has not yet seen the end of growth in the number of graduates; the annual numbers of graduates will rise by a further 60,000 in 1996/7.

An important issue is the graduate skills required by employers. For many jobs, employers require general competences – general academic skills (numeracy, information technology) and social skills (communications, social and interactive skills) – rather than specific academic knowledge. The Enterprise in Higher Education programme was introduced by the Employment Department to promote a shift towards the inculcation of such general competences. The employment market has yet to see the end of graduate growth. The 1993 intake to full-time and sandwich courses – the last during the period of growth – will not graduate until 1996 or 1997. They will enter a labour market that is changing. The Warwick University Institute of Employment Research (ED, 1993) forecasts employment growth to the year 2000 in higher level occupations (managers, professionals and technicians) which will benefit graduates and diplomates.

RESEARCH

Research within universities has also been subject to changes in recent years, as the government has implemented a policy to increase accountability and to reward assessed quality. However the changes have been more gradual than for teaching.

Research is funded under a 'dual support' system under which the Funding Councils fund the costs of infrastructure and of basic research, including the fixed costs of permanent academic staff and premises. Additional funding for projects is provided by the Research Councils which support direct costs and some overhead costs. UFC funding rose by 26 per cent from £535 million in 1989/90 to £673 million in 1992/3. In addition, PCFC distributed £15 million to polytechnics and colleges in 1991/2 and 1992/3. University research income from external sources rose by 165 per cent from £349 million in 1984/5 to £924 million in 1991/2 (DfE, 1994).

The 1991 White Paper (DES, 1991) set out the government's policy that:

- teaching and research funding should be separately identified;

- research funding should be 'allocated selectively to encourage institutions to concentrate on their strengths' (para 38).

Research assessment exercises were carried by the UGC and later the UFC in 1986, 1989 and 1992, with an increasingly refined methodology. The outcome of the 1992 exercise was regarded as broadly fair by universities, although there was some comment on the varying levels of funding in similar academic units (Johnstone, 1993). The characteristics of the 1992 exercise were:

- it covered all four UK countries;
- polytechnics and colleges were allowed to bid for the first time;
- institutions would select which 'research active' staff within departments to bid;
- research was rated on a five-point scale;
- the amount given depended on the quality rating (QR), the number of staff declared 'research active', the amount of contract research income (CR) and an element to develop research (DevR); and
- the assessment was split up into 72 academic units.

After the exercise, older universities received 91 per cent of the research funding in 1993/4, new universities 7 per cent and colleges 2 per cent (HEFCE, 1994a). The distribution of this new funding caused deep discussions in new universities and colleges on whether to give all the funds to the department which had earned them or to top slice and encourage research in other departments (McVicar, 1994).

The 1992 research assessment exercise resulted in a wide distribution of research funding (wider than for teaching funding). The biggest recipients fell into two main groups: Oxbridge and the biggest London colleges, and the older civic universities. Most of these are well represented in the more expensive medical, science and engineering research. There is evidence that most universities are now positioning themselves for the next assessment exercise in 1996 and seeking to recruit senior research staff especially in social sciences and humanities, where barriers to entry are low because they are a people business. While positions at the top of the research funding hierarchy are unlikely to change much, the positions in the middle order may be very different by the end of the decade.

A long-term consequence of research assessment may be to concentrate research in fewer universities. The American model of graduate schools has been seen as a means to focus not only postgraduate research education but also research effort as research is increasingly concentrated in a small number of 'research universities' within a mass higher education system (Phillips, 1994).

Running alongside the development of research assessment by successive Funding Councils have been changes in science research funding. The 1993 White Paper *Realising Our Potential: A Strategy for Science, Engineering and Technology* (OST, 1993) made several proposals that directly affect universities:

- a reorganization of the Research Councils, most importantly a split of the Science and Engineering Research Council into the Engineering and Physical Sciences Research Council and the Particle Physics and Astronomy Research Council;
- the creation of a technology foresight programme to identify emerging developments and inform government policy;
- a reorganization of postgraduate research training.

Changes are now also being made to the funding of economic and social research.

Funding for postgraduate research students is provided by the Research Councils and the training is carried out in universities; typically an award is made for three years for training leading to a PhD. The proposals for reorganizing research training (OST, 1994) envisage two stages: a Masters year which should provide both training in research methods and the development of specialist knowledge, followed by a PhD. The intention is that the 'research' Masters degree should be distinct from other Masters degrees and should be a qualification in its own right. There may be arrangements for 'recognizing' equivalent training in other degrees (eg, four-year undergraduate programmes leading to Masters degrees) and other forms of flexibility.

CONCLUSION

Higher education has changed since the mid-1980s; it has not simply grown. Much of it has changed its character. The range of backgrounds of students, the range of courses they undertake, and the range of types of universities and colleges means that much more choice is available to would-be students. Some universities and colleges have remained little affected, but most have been changed beyond recognition. The successful way that these changes have been organized is a tribute to the management skills of staff at all levels in universities and colleges.

The key to the future is to balance two factors: the need for the imaginative delivery of education opportunities to meet the needs of lifelong learning and the pressures to conform to traditional standards in teaching and learning. The prospects for the next few years is that quality rather than growth will make higher education more inward-looking and conservative. The swashbuckling entrepreneurialism of the early 1990s may have been a passing phase, and there may be a retreat to conservation. Let us hope not.

REFERENCES

CBI (1993) *Routes for Success – Careership*, London: Confederation of British Industry.

CVCP (1993) Review of Options for the Additional Funding of Higher Education, Report by London Economics for CVCP, London.

DES (1987) *Higher Education: Meeting the Challenge*, (Cm 114), London: HMSO.

DES (1991) *Higher Education: A New Framework*, (Cm 1541), London: HMSO.

DES/ED (1991) *Education and Training for the 21st Century*, (Cm 1536), London: HMSO.

DfE (1993) *Higher Quality and Choice: The Charter for Higher Education*, London: DfE.

DfE (1994) *The Government's Expenditure Plans 1994–95 to 1996–97*, (Cm 2510), London: HMSO.

ED (1993) *Labour Market and Skill Trends 1994/95*, London: Employment Department.

HEFCE (1993) *The Review of the Academic Year*, Bristol: Higher Education Funding Council for England.

HEFCE (1994a) *An Overview of Recent Developments in Higher Education in the UK*, January 1994, Bristol: Higher Education Funding Council for England.

HEFCE (1994b) *Assessment of the Quality of Higher Education: A Review and an Evaluation*, report by the Institute of Education, University of London, Bristol: the Higher Education Funding Council for England and Wales.

HEQC (1993) *Some Aspects of Higher Education Programmes in Further Education Institutions*, London: Higher Education Quality Council.

Johnstone, RJ (1993) 'Funding research: an exploration of inter-discipline variations', *Higher Education Quarterly*, 47, 4.

Lloyd, B (1992) 'Lifelong Learning: The real challenge for the 1990s, *Higher Education Policy*, 5, 4.

McVicar, M (1994) 'The 1992/93 research assessment exercise: the view from a former polytechnic', *Higher Education Quarterly*, 48, 1.

OST (1993) *Realising Our Potential: A Strategy for Science, Engineering and Technology*, (Cm 2250), London: HMSO.

OST (1994) *A New Structure for Postgraduate Research Training Supported by the Research Councils*, consultation paper, London: Office of Science and Technology.

PCFC (1990) *Performance Indicators: Report of Committee of Enquiry*, Bristol: Polytechnics and Colleges Funding Council.

PCFC (1992a) *Macro Performance Indicators*, Bristol: Polytechnics and Colleges Funding Council.

PCFC (1992b) *Polytechnics and Colleges Strategic Plans 1991–92 to 1995–96*, Bristol: Polytechnics and Colleges Funding Council.

Phillips, Sir David (1994) 'The research mission and research manpower', in *Universities in the Twenty-First Century: A Lecture Series*, London: National Commission on Education.

Roberts, D *et al* (1992) *Higher Education: The Student Experience*, Leeds: HEIST.

SBU (1993) *Student Satisfaction Survey Report*, London: South Bank University.

Smithers, A (1993) 'All Our Futures: Britain's Education Revolution', Channel Four Television.

UCE (1993) *The 1993 Report on the Student Experience at UCE*, University of Central England in Birmingham: Student Satisfaction Research Unit, Centre for the Study of Quality in HE.

INDEX